*Oh, great and just God, no man among us
knows what the sleeper knows, nor is it for us to judge
what lies between him and Thee.*
PRAYER AT THE FUNERAL OF A SUICIDE, IN WILLA CATHER, *MY ÁNTONIA*

*Almighty God, Father of mercies and giver of comfort:
Deal graciously, we pray, with all who mourn;
that, casting all their care on you, they may
know the consolation of your love; through Jesus Christ our Lord.
Amen.*
THE BOOK OF COMMON PRAYER

Grieving a Suicide

A Loved One's
Search
for Comfort,
Answers
& Hope

Albert Y. Hsu

InterVarsity Press
Downers Grove, Illinois

InterVarsity Press
P.O. Box 1400, Downers Grove, IL 60515-1426
World Wide Web: www.ivpress.com
E-mail: mail@ivpress.com

InterVarsity Press® is the book-publishing division of InterVarsity Christian Fellowship/USA®, a student movement active on campus at hundreds of universities, colleges and schools of nursing in the United States of America, and a member movement of the International Fellowship of Evangelical Students. For information about local and regional activities, write Public Relations Dept., InterVarsity Christian Fellowship/USA, 6400 Schroeder Rd., P.O. Box 7895, Madison, WI 53707-7895, or visit the IVCF website at <www.ivcf.org>.

All Scripture quotations, unless otherwise indicated, are taken from the Holy Bible, New International Version®. NIV®. Copyright ©1973, 1978, 1984 by International Bible Society. Used by permission of Zondervan Publishing House. All rights reserved.

While all of the stories and examples in this book come from real people and events, some names and identifying details have been altered to protect the privacy of the individuals involved.

Cover photograph: Joachim Heller/SuperStock

ISBN 0-8308-2318-2

Printed in the United States of America ∞

Library of Congress Cataloging-in-Publication Data

Hsu, Albert Y., 1972-
 Grieving a suicide: a loved one's search for comfort, answers & hope / Albert Y. Hsu.
  p. cm.
 ISBN 0-8308-2318-2 (pbk. : alk. paper)
  1. Bereavement—Religious aspects—Christianity. 2. Suicide—Religious
aspects—Christianity. 3. Consolation. I. Title.

BV4905.3 .H78 2002
248.8'66—dc21
                                                                2002017264

| P | 17 | 16 | 15 | 14 | 13 | 12 | 11 | 10 | 9 | 8 | 7 | 6 | 5 | 4 | 3 | 2 | 1 |
| Y | 16 | 15 | 14 | 13 | 12 | 11 | 10 | 09 | 08 | 07 | 06 | 05 | 04 | 03 | 02 |

IN MEMORY OF MY FATHER
TERRY TSAI-YUAN HSU

1939-1998

Contents

Introduction

For *Survivors*— the Other Victims of Suicide

One of my students once described her cousin's suicide and its continuing effects on his family by saying, "He didn't just take his own life; he took part of theirs too."
GILBERT MEILAENDER, *BIOETHICS*

*I*f you have experienced the suicide of a loved one, this book is for you.

Approximately a million people around the world kill themselves each year. In the United States over thirty-two thousand suicides take place annually—perhaps far more, since many suicides are disguised to look like accidents.

While suicides often take place in isolation, they are never unnoticed by others. There may be one primary victim, but as with a bomb thrown into a crowd of people, the collateral damage done to others nearby is massive. An individual suicide causes numerous other casualties—friends and family, the "other victims." Every suicide leaves behind at least six survivors, sometimes ten or more.

In most literature on the topic, "suicide survivor" refers to a loved one left behind by a suicide—husband, wife, parent, child, roommate, coworker, another family member, friend—not a person who has survived a suicide attempt. It is no coincidence that the term *survivor* is commonly applied to those who have experienced a horrible catastrophe of earth-shattering proportions. We speak of Holocaust survivors or of survivors of genocide, terrorism or war. So it is with those of us who survive a suicide. According to the American Psychiatric Association, "the level of stress resulting from the suicide of a loved one is ranked as catastrophic—equivalent to that of a concentration camp experience."[1]

Survivor suggests desperation, one who clings to life, but only barely. The TV show *Survivor* created an artificial environment in which a group of people was stranded in a remote location to fend for themselves. But their actual survival was never really in doubt; after all, there were camera crews, directors and production assistants on hand to chronicle their everyday experiences. Not so with the survivors of a true catastrophe, like a shipwreck or plane crash. These survivors do not have any guarantee of survival. Their lives hang in the balance. They may have survived an initial life-threatening crisis, but they face an ongoing, day-to-day challenge of survival with no assurance of safety, rescue or recovery.

Such is the case for survivors of suicide. We have experienced a trauma on par psychologically with the experience of soldiers in combat. In the aftermath, we simply don't know if we can endure the pain and anguish. Because death has struck so close to home, life itself seems uncertain. We don't know if we can go on from day to day. We wonder if we will be consumed by the same despair that claimed our loved one. At the very least, we know that our life will never be the same. If we go on living, we will do so as people who see the world very differently.

Shortly after my father's suicide, I purchased a dozen books on the topic. Most sat on my shelf unread for months: I discovered that I was unable to bring myself to read them. Many times I would pick one up and attempt to read a few pages, only to abandon it when tears clouded my vision.

If this is your experience as well, that's fine. You certainly do not need to read this book straight through from cover to cover. In fact, you may not be able to. Read only what you can handle. Feel free to skip around and go directly to chapters that you think may be helpful to you. The chapters in the first part of the book deal more directly with the immediate grief experience, whereas the second part attempts to answer the haunting questions that suicides present. The third section offers further reflection on living one's life following a suicide.

Some things I read early in my own grieving made no sense to me at the time. They seemed too trite, like simplistic pat answers. My emotions were probably too raw then, my grief too fresh. Now that some time has passed, things make a little more sense. So if some of my observations are of no help to you right now, I apologize in advance and pray that I have not added to your grief. I do not pretend to offer the authoritative word on this topic, but I hope this book can be a companion through your experience.

I grew up in Minnesota, a state known for frigid winters and heavy snowfall. The wind-chill factor falls so far below zero that merely taking a breath brings sharp pain to your lungs and makes your nostrils freeze up. I remember childhood blizzards when I looked out the window and couldn't even see the end of the driveway. The dark skies, icy streets and arctic winds made it nearly impossible to travel anywhere or even to see where to go. These storms are dangerous. Without proper protection, people caught outside can die.

But eventually the storms subside, leaving an altered landscape. Familiar landmarks have disappeared under a cover of crystal white. It can be hazardous to venture outdoors after a new snow. Many slip and fall on the ice, breaking hips or wrists. Every year some people have heart attacks while shoveling their driveways. Even walking through the snow can be risky. If the top layer of the snow is crusted over with ice, the surface appears deceptively solid. But with one misplaced step, your leg can break through the crust and sink up to your thigh.

Soon enough, however, shovels and snowblowers emerge, and gradually the sidewalks reappear, marked by the bootprints of those who clear new paths. It's always easier to walk through snowdrifts if you place your feet in the footsteps of those who trudged through earlier.

Survivors of suicide can feel as if they are caught in a winter storm of epic proportions. The road ahead looks bleak and daunting. It may not seem to lead anywhere, or you may seem to be going in circles. You may feel as if you are frozen in place. You may think that you'll die. But wherever you are on the journey, know that the path you tread is one that others have trod. I hope this book provides you with some protection in the storm, that it will guard your heart and soul during a time of terrible agony. May it provide you with some tracks to follow to make your way through.

Part I

When *Suicide* Strikes

*Suicide doesn't end pain. It only lays it on
the broken shoulders of the survivors.*
ANNE-GRACE SCHEININ

1

Shock

*I*t was a Thursday morning when I heard.

I had been getting ready for work. I was looking forward to the weekend because my wife and I were planning on attending a friend's wedding in Minnesota and visiting my parents while we were in the state. In preparation, I gathered a few things to bring with us, including some enlargements of our wedding photos for my mother and a book for my dad.

I also had a copy of our wedding video for my parents. Ellen and I had gotten married nine months prior. The video was unlabeled, so I put it in the VCR and played the first few seconds to make sure it was the right tape. I caught a glimpse of my mother being ushered down the aisle and the back of my father's head as he started to follow. I stopped the video and put it back in its case.

Then the phone rang. I couldn't think who would be calling us so early in the morning. I told Ellen I would get it.

The voice on the line seemed unearthly, a combination of howls and sobs. Who was this? Was it a wrong number? Then I realized that it was my mother, in hysterics. Her voice was overwhelmed with emotion, terror, grief.

"Daddy killed himself!" she wailed.

"What?" I asked. "What happened? Mom, what happened!"

But she had left the phone, and I could hear her sobbing in the background. Daddy? Daddy who? *My* dad? Ellen looked at me with a puzzled expression on her face, and I gestured for her to pick up the extension.

"Mom? Mom! Are you there?" I yelled into the phone. "Mom!"

For several agonizing seconds we heard little on the other end of the line. Then she was back and told me that she had found Dad's body that morning. I asked if she had called the police. They were there now, she said. She left the phone again, evidently to talk to somebody. Then a neighbor's voice came on the line, and she told me what little she knew.

"Albert, your father strangled himself," the neighbor said. "Your mom needs you to come home." Then she had to hang up because the police needed the phone, but she said that someone would call us back soon.

I hung up the phone in shock. Ellen, who had been listening on the extension, came over to me and held me. She started to cry, and an unfeeling numbness seeped through my body. I sat down on the couch, not quite able to grasp what had happened. I couldn't wrap my mind around the concept. *Suicide?* My dad?

Ellen called our workplace to tell them what had happened, that we would be leaving for Minnesota right away. She called our alma mater and left a message for one of the professors, whom we had planned to visit that weekend, to let him know of the unexpected change of plans. She also left a message for the college faculty, asking for prayer for my family. She then called our church and left a message for our pastor.

She started to pack. I still sat on the couch, not wanting to believe that this was really taking place. Was this real? Had this actually happened? My father, age fifty-eight, had had a stroke three months prior, just before Thanksgiving. He had lost some motor function in the left side of his body and had begun a rehabilitation and therapy program. He had become very depressed after the stroke, and I knew he had been having a hard time coming to terms with the loss of autonomy and control over his own body. A month earlier, we had heard some encouraging news that things seemed to be going better. But now, suddenly, he was gone.

My mom called again a few minutes later. In a calmer voice she told me that my dad had attempted suicide a week earlier. She had wanted to tell me when it happened, but my dad didn't want me to know. He hadn't wanted me to worry about him, to be burdened by that kind of knowledge. "I was going to tell you this weekend," Mom said sadly.

She asked if we would be coming home, and I told her we were packing. I said we'd see her that afternoon, and we hung up.

As we packed, we got more phone calls. A professor from our alma mater called and told us that the campus would be praying for us. Our pastor, Matthew, called and asked if he could come over to see us. We said that we were about to leave, but we'd be stopping by our office on our way out of town. Ellen's supervisor called to let us know that the company would be praying for us that morning.

Within an hour we had gathered our things for the drive home. I packed the wedding video, which my father would now never see. Before we left our apartment, I saw the book I had planned to bring to my dad. I placed it back on the shelf. I had thought about giving it to him some months ago but hadn't gotten around to it. Now he would never read it, or anything else. Now it was too late.

The Shock of Discovery

"The initial impact of discovery scars us forever," declares one suicide survivor.[1] Some survivors have the horrible experience of witnessing the actual suicide. In the midst of a heated argument, one young woman's husband shouted "I'll show you!" just before shooting himself.[2] Another man, in the process of a divorce, told his wife that he could not live without her. She watched in horror as he put a gun to his head and pulled the trigger. "I don't think I can ever get over this," she says.

Others have the shock of discovering the body and thereafter are haunted by images of blood and death. Pictures are seared in our memory. "I will never be able to get the image of him, lying on the floor with a hose to the gas and a trash bag over his head, out of my mind," says a survivor.

Those of us who hear about the discovery after the fact, while spared the graphic memory of our loved one's act, nonetheless are plagued by our imaginations. We wonder what the scene looked like. We envision the final moments. Whether we witnessed the death or not, we replay images over and over in our head, like a movie on a loop that we can't turn off.

Survivors of suicide have a variety of initial reactions to the news. Some shut down emotionally. "My world went black" is how Stephanie describes how she felt upon hearing of her mother's suicide. "I felt ice-cold."[3] Others feel physical upheaval, as if punched in the gut. We might be overwhelmed by uncontrollable wails or sobs, or we may experience rage or anger. We may experience denial, like the mother in the movie *Dead Poets Society,* who cries, "He's all right! He's all right!" upon discovering her son's body.

Another common response is to attribute the death to something other than suicide. If the cause of death is ambiguous, survivors may call it an accident. We might think, *She didn't mean to take all those pills; it must have been an accidental overdose.* Or we may even hope that the death was actually a murder rather than a suicide. Perhaps some unknown intruder killed our loved one and staged it to look like a suicide. After Natalie's mother jumped off an eighteen-story building, Natalie found the idea of suicide so unbelievable that she wondered if some unknown assailant had pushed her off.[4] If we could find an alternative explanation for the death, we could blame the death on accidental forces or an external villain, not our loved one.

Sometimes in the face of tragic loss we mistakenly believe we should not be mired in such feelings as grief or sorrow. Counselor Stephen Arterburn calls this "the myth of instant peace."

> I have heard people who have lost children, spouses, fortunes, and dreams say that they have this "wonderful peace" just moments after they hear the awful news. What they have is shock, not peace! Shock is a natural reaction designed to protect us, to cushion the reality and depth of our pain and other feelings. Those who profess instant peace will suffer a troubled future full of greater pain than the original loss and disappointment.[5]

While some degree of denial is common in most kinds of catastrophic loss, denial usually serves only as a temporary shock absorber to prepare us for future grief work. It is a psychological buffer zone to help us with the immediacy of the trauma but should not become a permanent dwelling place for our grief. "Denial puts off what should be faced," writes Gerald Sittser.[6] Because those who dwell in denial actually avoid pain rather than confront it, healing can be cut short. Denial may be a natural starting point for the grief experience, but it is only part of the journey.

Whatever your initial reaction to the news of your loved one's suicide, know that there is no "right" or "wrong" way to respond. How you feel or what you think at the time of the tragic news is immediate and visceral, and it usually need not be evaluated, modified or self-censored. It simply *is*. Granted, some survivors may need to be protected from responding in ways that may be destructive to themselves or others. When we receive the bad news, our minds and bodies respond with a defense mechanism, a survival instinct to keep us going. Because of individual circumstances and personalities, all of us will respond in different ways, yet our various experiences will have much in common with those of other survivors.

When I got the news, I felt numb. The news came as a shock, but not really as a surprise. Because of my dad's depression in the previous months, his suicide "made sense." I could understand in my head why he would want to take his own life. But that rational assessment did little to diminish the enormous emptiness I felt within my chest. I couldn't grasp the reality of his death, and I certainly hadn't seen it coming.

What are we to do when we are in the initial stages of shock? Shock incapacitates some survivors while it mobilizes others into action. Among the friends and family who have been left behind, some may be able to make decisions while others find themselves in a daze. I was grateful for the ways my wife helped me function in the immediate minutes and hours after I heard the news. If you sense that you can act with some degree of clarity, do what you can to help others. If you find yourself at a loss, feel free to tell someone, "I don't think I can handle anything right now. I need you to take care of some things for me."

We Are Not Alone
Suicide bisects your life with a thick dark line. Everything is divided into "before" and "after." Overnight my mother became a widow. My brother and I became fatherless. Instantly everything had changed.

Against our will, those of us who have experienced the suicide of a loved one have become part of a unique grieving community. Our particular kind of grief is incomprehensible to many, since death by suicide is radically different from death by car accident, heart attack or old age. "We are like members of a secret society," one author writes.[7] It is a society that no one wants to be a part of, one that we wish we had not been initiated into.

If you are a survivor of suicide, you are not alone. Every day countless others experience the same horrible heartache. Millions across the country and around the world have known the searing pain, the gnawing anguish, the unanswered questions of a suicide.

Some months after my father's death, I came across a book by a suicide survivor that described her experience. A month after her husband's suicide, Carla went to a local church's suicide survivors support group for the first time. She could not imagine what she might encounter, perhaps a roomful of crazy, disturbed people. She had no idea what it would be like to talk about her husband's death with complete strangers.

She approached the meeting room, marked with a sign reading "A Safe Place." There she found a group of normal-looking people drinking coffee and eating cookies, making small talk and exchanging pleasantries. Carla was sure she was in the wrong place. How could these people know anything of her trauma and grief? She started to leave but was encouraged to stay.

As the meeting began, the facilitator welcomed the group and asked people to introduce themselves and say why they were there.

"My name is Ray," one man began. "My brother hung himself two years ago at Bear Mountain State Park. He was thirty-six, my younger brother."

"My name is Elizabeth. My father shot himself last year on Thanksgiving Day. It was two hours before we were going to eat." Elizabeth began to cry.

"I'm Ivan. My son jumped in front of the subway four months, two weeks, and three days ago." He had been a high school sophomore.

"My name is Hal. I found my fourteen-year-old daughter in the bathtub with her wrists slit on July 8, 1989 . . ."

And so it continued. A heart surgeon had jumped out a window. A police detective shot himself the day before he retired. A mother overdosed on pills on her seventy-fifth birthday. A twin sister strangled herself with her bed sheets while under suicide watch at a psychiatric hospital. A wife turned on the car in the garage and died from carbon monoxide fumes.

Finally it was Carla's turn, and in tears she said, "My name is Carla, and this is my first meeting. It's my husband's birthday today; he would have been forty-four. He killed himself four weeks ago. He was a doctor, so he injected himself intravenously with some heavy-duty anesthetic. Up until tonight, I didn't know there were so many other people who could understand what I was talking about."[8]

As I read about Carla's experience, something resonated within me. It was horrifying to read about all the different ways people had killed themselves, and it seemed morbid for all these relatives to be talking about their loved ones' deaths. Yet, strangely, I found it tremendously reassuring. By reading other people's stories, I realized that I was not alone. Others had gone through similar experiences and had felt the same emotions.

Later, as I began to share my own experience and grief with those around me, I discovered—to my surprise—that a number of my friends and coworkers had walked this same difficult road, had experienced the suicide of a loved one. They told me, in various ways, "I'm a survivor too."

Many of those who resort to suicide have felt utterly alone in their depression or pain and have believed that nobody else knows how they feel. The fact is that many others share the same thoughts and struggles, and if they had known of others in their shoes, they might have found the hope to go on. Survivors, likewise, must not believe the lie that nobody knows how we feel. We are not alone in this trauma. Others have experienced the same tragedy and have weathered the storm. They have been able to go on. We can too.

Turmoil

Suicide carries in its aftermath a level of confusion and devastation that is, for the most part, beyond description.
PSYCHOLOGIST KAY REDFIELD JAMISON,
NIGHT FALLS FAST

I keep thinking that he's not really dead," Ellen said. "That maybe they're wrong, that he's going to come back."

I nodded in agreement. It simply did not seem real. Until that time I had rarely thought about death. It was only an abstract concept, held off at a distance. I had figured that I would deal with it eventually, when my parents were older. But death had violently ambushed me. What was I supposed to do? How was I supposed to respond? Nobody had prepared me for anything like this.

As we left town, we stopped at the office to drop off some things. I couldn't bring myself to go inside and face my friends and coworkers, so Ellen ran in. I later learned that our coworkers had called together an impromptu prayer meeting in the company lunchroom to pray for me and my family.

Ellen came back with our pastor, Matthew, and his wife, Kim, who had gone to the office to catch us before we left town. They stood by our car to express their condolences and pray for us. I don't remember anything of what Matthew prayed, but I remember seeing tears running down Kim's face. She didn't even know my father. Why was she crying? Why wasn't I?

During the six-and-a-half-hour drive to Minnesota, I couldn't stop thinking about my dad. Random memories whirled through my mind. I last saw him over Thanksgiving, three months prior. We had visited him several times in the hospital, where he was recovering from the stroke. He had looked older and more frail; his left side wasn't working properly, and he shuffled when he walked. Though he was slightly depressed at his physical state, he had seemed very happy to see us. I learned some things about him I had never known before, like the fact that he didn't like the smell of new dollar bills when they come fresh out of the ATM. He actually stashed new bills around his office at work until the odor went away, so they wouldn't make his wallet smell funny. He asked about my life and career and said that he'd like to help us with a down payment for a house when the time came. He thanked us for visiting and hugged us when we left. It was some of the best time I had ever spent with my dad. I didn't realize then that it would be the last time I would see him alive.

A few weeks before his death I had talked to him on the phone for what would be the last time. He had said very little. "Well, I'm feeling pretty low," he had said. "Sorry I don't have much to say." I remembered thinking that I had never heard my dad so sad before. He seemed so vulnerable and weak, so unlike the independent, strong-willed, self-made man I'd known as my father. For the first time, perhaps, I recognized that my dad had deep fears and worries. I just didn't know how consuming his despair had become.

We arrived at my parents' home late that afternoon. It was winter in Minnesota, so the ground was covered with snow, and gray skies cast a bleak pallor over the house. Several cars were parked in the driveway and on the street, signaling that friends and neighbors were with my mother.

"Mom, I'm home," I said as I opened the front door. I saw her sitting in the living room with some people I recognized and others who were unfamiliar. Her face seemed oddly blank, as if a torrent of emotions had left her drained. She came over to embrace me somewhat awkwardly.

"Dad loved you very much," she said to me. "If he had been in his right mind, he wouldn't have done this." I wasn't sure whether to agree or not, so I just hugged her.

Mom sent me to pick up Ed, my younger brother, from church, where the youth pastor, Scott, said he'd be willing to help out with funeral arrangements. Back home, the phone rang constantly, as relatives and friends called to express their condolences to my mom. Over and over she had to recount what had happened.

What I pieced together was that following his stroke, my father had begun to show all the symptoms of clinical depression. In the last few weeks, he had lost sense of perspective and constantly felt like a failure, guilty, hopeless. My mom had removed firearms and other weapons from the house, fearing that he would hurt himself. Then Dad tried to kill himself with a belt. Mom found out and got him to the hospital for several days of supervision.

He had been back home for a few days when he told Mom that he wanted to be left alone for the night, that he didn't want her to come in or disturb him. Evidently he took a coat hanger from the closet, stretched it open, hooked it on the headboard of the bed and placed his head through it. He lay down on the bed and let his body weight pull the hanger against his neck, strangling him. I had no idea that anyone could kill himself that way. It spoke to me both of my father's determination and of his desperation.

The next few days were a maelstrom of activity. As the eldest son, I did my best to act responsibly, helping with funeral arrangements, attending to guests, cleaning out the refrigerator. But through it all I wandered in a confusing mix of emotion and heartache. I didn't know how I felt. I wasn't sure I could function. Each day was filled with uncertainty and a sense of dread.

Grief and Trauma

"In grief nothing 'stays put,'" writes C. S. Lewis. "One keeps on emerging from a phase, but it always recurs. Round and round. Everything repeats. Am I going in circles, or dare I hope I am on a spiral?"[1]

Much has been written about "stages of grief." The most widely used framework has five basic phases: denial, anger, bargaining, depression and acceptance.[2] Another source proposes ten stages: shock, expression of emotion, depression and loneliness, physical distress, panic, guilt, anger and resentment, resistance, hope, and affirmation of reality.[3]

But grief is rarely so clear or so simple. The fact that counselors and researchers plot out different kinds of grief patterns suggests that people grieve differently and experience different cycles of emotions. Our grief recovery processes are not so easily charted. One author did not find the idea of stages of grief helpful because "for one thing, I have still not moved beyond these stages, and I am not sure I ever will." He still finds himself angry at times, in denial at others. The problem with seeing grief in stages, he says, "is that it raises the false expectation that we go through them only once. Again, that has not been true for me. I have revisited them again and again."[4] Identifying stages of grief may provide a general idea of the kinds of patterns we might undergo, but our actual day-to-day experience can be volatile and erratic.

This is especially true in cases of catastrophic loss, like suicide. The grief that suicide survivors experience is described by psychologists as "complicated grief" or "complicated bereavement." *Grief* usually refers to a normal, anticipated loss, such as death by old age or a long illness. But complicated grief involves an additional trauma, such as suicide or murder. Counselors Mel Laurenz and Daniel Green define *grief* as "the natural, expected reaction to a loss." *Trauma,* on the other hand, is defined as "the experience of something shocking happening to someone (physically or psychologically) that produces some kind of inner injury and affects the person's ability to function in normal ways."[5]

Those of us who experience complicated bereavement are actually grappling with *two* realities, grief *and* trauma. Grief is normal; trauma is not. The combination of circumstances is like a vicious one-two punch. We are grieving the death of our loved one, *and* we are reeling from the trauma of the suicide. The first is difficult enough; the second may seem unbearable.

Suicide heightens the agony of loss. Different kinds of loss are grieved differently. The loss of a child, for instance, brings a different sort of grief than the loss of a spouse or an elderly parent. Each kind of death raises its own issues. A teen's death brings feelings of regret that a life of budding potential was cut short; the death of a wife or husband may leave the surviving spouse struggling with the challenges of widowhood and single parenting. Each of these losses is difficult even in the most "normal" of circumstances; suicide complicates and intensifies each grief. What would already be a heartbreaking teen death becomes even more tragic as a teen suicide. How a family grieves for a teen's suicide may look very different from grief over a grandfather's suicide.

Traumatic grief is not a linear process, a straight path mapped out from one starting point to a final destination. Rather, it is a journey filled with twists and turns, unexpected detours and dead ends that force us back over ground we thought we had already covered. Often several different, overlapping emotions may assault us at once, and we find ourselves caught in cycles of good days and bad.

The Emotional Whirlwind

The word I use to describe our experience of this combination of grief and trauma is *turmoil*. Following a suicide, we find ourselves in severe emotional and perhaps physical turmoil as our feelings and thoughts fly in all directions. We may discover that we are experiencing contradictory emotions at once, such as a melancholy sadness—normal grief—along with violent outrage at the trauma of suicide.

Here are some categories of turmoil that suicide survivors go through. They are listed in no particular order, since they may occur at any time and do not necessarily fit any prescribed pattern for stages of grief.

Shock, disbelief and numbness. C. S. Lewis writes that grief "feels like being mildly drunk, or concussed. There is a sort of invisible blanket between the world and me. I find it hard to take in what anyone says."[6]

"The immediate response to suicide is total disbelief," writes a suicide survivor. "The act itself is so incomprehensible that we enter into a state where we feel unreal and disconnected."[7]

The days right after a suicide are filled with confusion. We are caught up in the whirlwind of funeral preparations and decisions, talking to strangers like police officers as well as close friends and relatives, sorting through legal and financial matters. It leaves us bewildered. We hope that it's all a bad dream, a temporary alternate reality that we only need to endure for a while before we return to the real universe.

In our disbelief and numbness, we often shut down any emotions that come close to happiness or joy. We approach life with dead seriousness. We avoid TV sitcoms because we find none of the jokes funny. How can people laugh when this world is so painful? How can anything be funny anymore? We feel as if we will never smile again.

Distraction. After a suicide it is often difficult to concentrate. In the weeks afterward, I sometimes found myself sitting at my desk staring at the computer screen for an hour or more, unable to think about the tasks before me. I would walk around not knowing where I was going or what I was doing. In the middle of meetings, church services or even personal conversations I would zone out and then "come back" to realize that I had not heard what had been said for the past several minutes.

Friends of survivors may need an extra measure of patience in the early days of grief. Survivors may find themselves apologizing frequently, saying things like "I'm sorry, could you say that again? I didn't catch what you said." It's not that our hearing is going bad—it's that traumatic grief has caused an inability to focus.

Sorrow and despair. Tears may be uncontrollable. Deep sadness can linger for weeks, leaving us emotionally and physically exhausted. Survivors often fall into a state of melancholy and depression following a suicide. In some ways we may unconsciously identify with the hopelessness that precipitated our loved one's death. We may lack the energy to get out of bed in the morning. We may feel as if all our daily activity is meaningless.

Shortly after my father's death, my wife talked to a close friend who had been struggling with depression. Her friend confessed that she had drunk some toxic materials but had vomited them up.

When Ellen told me this, I suddenly burst into tears. "Why does the world have to be so sad?" I wailed, overwhelmed with a sudden sense of despair. Just hearing that someone else was feeling suicidal was enough to trigger grief in me all over again.

Rejection and abandonment. "It is the most denigrating form of rejection," one survivor writes. "Those of us who have been deserted by suicide are left with the rage of that desertion."[8] Suicide feels like a total dismissal, the cruelest possible way a person could tell us that they are leaving us behind. Spouses of suicides, in particular, often feel as if the decision is a personal rejection.[9] It is like the ultimate divorce, punctuated with the darkest of exclamation points. "I'm leaving you! Forever!" That's what a suicide declares to us.

So we feel abandoned. Our sense of self-worth is crippled. All our doubts and insecurities are magnified a hundredfold; if we felt unlovable before, now the fact of suicide only seems to confirm our suspicions. In my weaker moments, I would think, *I thought my dad cared about me. I thought he was proud of me. But now I see I was only kidding myself. If he had thought I was anything worthwhile, he wouldn't have left me this way.*

This is one reason that we survivors imagine other explanations for our loved one's death. "An accidental death or even murder does not carry the stigma and sense of abandonment that suicide does. It is easier, after all, to accept that someone one loves was taken away than that he or she chose to leave."[10]

Failure. When a teenager takes his or her own life, the parents may believe that the suicide confirms their failure in parenting. Not only must they grapple with the sense that their child has rejected them in the worst way possible, they feel as if they have failed. *If only we were better parents,* they think, *this wouldn't have happened.* And now the fact of the suicide seems a public declaration of parental dysfunction and defeat. One mother felt as though her car had a huge sign on it reading, "My son committed suicide. I am a failure."[11]

Feelings of failure may surface any time a survivor had a caretaking role. Healthcare professionals, counselors, pastors and other caregivers may feel a sense of failure if a patient, client or parishioner dies by suicide. My mother, a registered nurse, was taking care of my father during his stroke rehabilitation and depression. His suicide made her feel as if her caregiving efforts had failed.

Perhaps a quarter to a half of clinical therapists will experience the suicide of a client sometime during their career. They may go through endless reviews of a case file, asking, "What did I miss?" They may encounter family members who are angry at them for "blowing it."[12] "Therapists experience many of the same responses—the questioning, the anger, the guilt—that other survivors do. Moreover, a patient's suicide leaves the therapist with a host of questions about responsibility, competence, and even professional identity."[13]

Guilt and regret. Joan's son came home one day after an argument and screamed, "I'm sick of people blowing me off. I'm sick of it, I'm sick of it." He went up to his room while Joan stayed downstairs, watching TV. Then she heard the gunshot.

Now Joan wonders whether she could have prevented the suicide if she had gone upstairs to talk to him. "I feel the most guilt because I was the one who said that guns could come into the house. My husband did not want them in the house. . . . If I had not let the guns in the house, this never would have happened. I feel more guilt about that than anything."[14]

Many survivors feel a sense of responsibility for the loved one's death. We are haunted by an endless procession of "what ifs" and "if onlys." A wife says, "Like most survivors, I was haunted by the infinite regrets that are woven into the fabric of suicide. I would replay the chronology of events leading up to Harry's death, searching for lost opportunities to reverse the inevitable outcome."[15] What if I had been there? What if she had not been alone for the weekend? If only I had checked up on him that night. If only I had called a doctor sooner. If only, if only, if only.

"My sister slit her wrists after breaking up with her boyfriend," says Amanda, a twenty-three-year-old graduate student. "The night she died, there was a message from her on my answering machine asking me to call. I was tired and decided to phone back in the morning. I'll never know what would have happened if I had spoken to her. I keep thinking of her waiting for me and my just sleeping as she was bleeding to death in her bathtub."[16]

My father killed himself just two days before Ellen and I were going to visit him. I have a gnawing sense that he didn't want us to see him in his debilitated, depressed condition. Did the anticipation of my visit precipitate his suicide? If I had not made plans to see him, would he have not killed himself?

I have no answers to these questions. It is too easy to give in to the temptation of playing infinite alternate scenarios in my head, in which something different happens that changes history. I must deal with the reality that for whatever reason, my father took his own life. I will never know whether my impending visit forced his hand. After all, alternative scenarios are no more encouraging. What if he had waited to kill himself until after my visit? Would I then blame myself even more, telling myself that I should have done something during my visit to save him?

Our feelings of regret and guilt may seem overwhelming, but they eventually subside as we realize that the death was not our fault. The person who takes his or her own life by suicide is the one who is ultimately responsible, not us. One survivor says, "Only as I began to accept the idea that my husband's choice to kill himself was his alone did the powerful grip of the what-ifs of his suicide begin to loosen."[17]

Shame. Beyond the combination of normal grief and traumatic grief, survivors of suicide suffer an additional insult to injury—the societal stigma that surrounds suicide. It may be relatively easy to tell a friend or coworker that a person died in a car accident, or of leukemia; it can be very difficult to form the words, "She killed herself." It is something that we are ashamed of and that others find shameful. Many people see suicide as a sign of weakness and failure. We are afraid of what others will think of our loved one, or of us, if we tell them that the cause of death is suicide.

Even several years after the fact, I often find it difficult to tell others that my dad died by suicide. If someone I don't know very well asks about my dad's death, I may point to a secondary cause: "He had a stroke." Which is true, of course. I avoid mentioning that he survived the stroke and that the stroke led to a depression that triggered the suicide. If I feel more comfortable explaining the situation, I may say, "He took his own life."

Not only do we feel abandoned by the one who died, we may also find ourselves alienated, shunned by others who are uncomfortable with the fact of the suicide.[18] Margaret Atwood, in her novel *The Blind Assassin,* describes the stigma and blame that haunts survivors of suicide:

> Only one corpse in the river so far this year, a drug-ridden young woman from Toronto. . . . She had relatives here, an aunt, an uncle. Already they're the objects of narrow sideways looks, as if they had something to do with it; already they've assumed the cornered, angry air of the consciously innocent. I'm sure they're blameless, but they're alive, and whoever's left alive gets blamed. That's the rule in things like this. Unfair, but there it is.[19]

This kind of blame and stigma attaches itself to those surrounding a suicide. After a schoolteacher killed himself by jumping out of a twenty-seventh-story window, his class's students began to be avoided and ignored by other students, "almost like pariahs contaminated with the unpleasantness of suicide."[20]

Anger, rage and hatred. "One night, I parked at the lake and I yelled what I really felt at him," one survivor writes. "I wanted to shake his limp body back alive—violently shake him. I wanted to kill him for killing himself. How could he! How could he reject me so vehemently?"[21]

Anger is a very common emotion after a suicide. We feel that our loved one's action was utterly selfish, and we are angry at them for leaving us to clean up their mess. Suicide is particularly traumatizing because we do not know how to resolve our hurt and outrage. If it had been a murder, we could grieve for the victim and vent our rage at the murderer. But in the case of suicide, the victim *is* the murderer. And so we are conflicted. We may even hate our loved one for doing this to our loved one. We grieve the suicide and rage against him simultaneously.

"Anger is normal," bereavement counselor Laure Janus says. "I see lots of people in cemeteries yelling at gravestones."

Anxiety and fear. After a suicide we may become fearful that such a tragedy could happen again. What was once unthinkable now is within the realm of possibility. One survivor writes,

> Suicide was always something that other people did; it never happened to "normal" families like mine. Now I believe that anyone is capable of doing it. Recently, a friend came over for dinner and asked to use the bathroom to wash up. She was in there for what seemed a very long time and I became convinced that she must be killing herself. I started pounding frantically on the door, certain she was dead. My friend came running out of the bathroom, looking at me as if I were crazy. Obviously, suicide is never far from my mind. It happened once, and I keep waiting for it to happen again.[22]

Since we have lost a loved one in such a sudden and traumatic way, other similar losses seem likely, even inevitable. I now have a recurring fear that I will wake up one morning to find that my wife has suddenly died. Such abandonment fears can be long-lasting. One woman who lost a sibling to suicide reports that even thirty years later she continues to have irrational fears that a loved one will leave her.

"The most frightening part of suicide is its reminder that we are none of us so far from it," writes one author.[23] Once a suicide happens, we realize that we and others are far more vulnerable to despair and self-destructiveness than we had thought. We fear that we may be prone to taking our own life due to shared genetics and family environment. For parents who have lost a child to suicide, "unbridled terror that another child might also commit suicide is common, as is overprotectiveness of the surviving children."[24]

Paralysis. A few months after my father's suicide, the phone rang as I was getting ready for work one morning. I froze. The last time I had answered a phone call at that time of day, it was my mom with the news of my dad's death. Now I relived the dread and trauma.

Since the suicide, we had gotten a caller ID unit. I approached the phone, and the screen registered the name of a local medical clinic. It turned out to be a coordinator at the doctor's office, calling to confirm an appointment for a routine visit.

I breathed a tremendous sigh of relief, disconcerted that a simple phone call had triggered such an anxiety-filled reaction. It made me wonder if I would now react that way whenever I received an early-morning phone call.

Sleeplessness. The mental turmoil of grief makes us long for rest and reprieve. Unfortunately, another common experience of grievers is the sleepless night. We lie awake, with our thoughts flying in all directions, yearning for respite, but the inner turbulence deprives us of the oblivion of sleep. Quite often now I wake at three or four in the morning and toss and turn, unable to fall back asleep. I'm left alone with my thoughts, often about the suicide. There is nothing restful about thinking about a loved one's death over and over. And it can be hard to explain to others. What are we to say, that we spend all night thinking about suicide and death?

These nights come all too frequently, and they can be dreadful. Sometimes I pray for the ability to fall back asleep, only to be haunted by troubling, irrational dreams or outright nightmares. More often I simply get up and find a book to read to distract myself and turn my thoughts elsewhere. Or I may journal for a while, to get all the disturbing thoughts out of my head. Gradually the new day emerges, and my mind is eased.

Relief. We may find that our grief is mixed with a sense of relief. About half of suicides are at least somewhat expected due to ongoing depression or patterns of self-destructive behavior.[25] In our sadness, we are shocked to discover that we are glad it's all over. While these feelings are authentic, they are troubling to survivors. After all, our loved one has just died; how can we be happy that he or she is gone?

"Feeling relieved following the suicide of a loved one is not uncommon," writes survivor Eric Marcus. "For example, if a loved one had struggled with chronic depression or schizophrenia, had been in and out of hospitals, or had been abusing drugs and/or alcohol, his or her death is likely to be something of a relief."[26]

The suicide, though it introduces a whole new set of issues, brings resolution to others. Parents may be relieved that they will no longer have painful arguments with their troubled teen. Others may feel relief that their terminally ill relative will no longer languish in the hospital. The death, though tragic, means that some fears will not be realized. One survivor spoke of how their family even "celebrated" the fact that their loved one was no longer suffering the pain of terminal illness.

Nevertheless, relief is a troubling emotion. We feel that we should not take relief at such a tragic circumstance, as if we are glad our loved one is gone because his or her absence benefits us in some way. We feel guilty. It feels selfish, because the survivors experience relief while the suicide has paid the price.

Self-destructive thoughts and feelings. One danger of being a suicide survivor is the possibility of falling into suicidal despair. Survivors generally have an increased risk of suicidal behavior and depressive episodes.[27] Almost all suicide survivors have at least fleeting thoughts of their own suicide. Counselors Ann Smolin and John Guinan say, "Thoughts of suicide may recur for some time as the reality of what has happened becomes real to you. We strongly urge all survivors to remove weapons or other means of self-destruction from their homes."[28]

Most of my friends and colleagues perceive me as a normally upbeat, high-energy person. They are often surprised if I appear downcast. But those who know me best know that I have a melancholic side, prone to introspection. Sometimes that melancholic temperament can lead to self-destructive thoughts and feelings.

They have come at the oddest times. As I prepare dinner in the kitchen, cutting chicken breasts, I might morbidly realize how easy it would be to slash myself with the knife. Clipping coupons from the paper, I might have a bizarre thought about what it would feel like to stab myself in the head with the scissors. I get freaked out by sharp objects because they make me realize how fragile our bodies are, how simple it is to draw blood, how easily our lives could be extinguished.

Some survivors physically retrace the suicide's final steps and try to visualize the final act. One man whose son jumped off a fourteen-story building found himself imagining what his son would have experienced. He found himself preoccupied with staring out windows and even leaning over balconies. One evening, alone at work, he nearly stepped out a window to his own death before he overcame the compulsion. Thereafter he made sure he was never left alone in the office.

Another survivor, trying to understand why her daughter shot herself, would stand by the bathroom sink and stare in the mirror, imagining her daughter's final thoughts. One day she retrieved the same gun that her daughter had used and actually put it to her head, just as her daughter had done. Somehow she stopped herself from pulling the trigger. She was so scared by her actions that she gave away the gun to remove the temptation.[29]

If you have such inclinations, please find help! Tell a friend; call your pastor, a crisis hotline or even the police. Do not compound the tragedy of your loved one's suicide by killing yourself. Be aware that despair may threaten you. Take precautions against it.

Facing the Turmoil

How do we sort through these conflicting emotions? Is there any way to cope? Perhaps the starting point is to understand that most of our turmoil is to be expected. "Most suicide survivors are more 'emotional' than those experiencing normal grief," writes John Hewett in his book *After Suicide*. "What may seem abnormal or 'hysterical' to you is actually quite normal for people in your situation."[30]

At first we may not be able to do much more than just feel the trauma. This is how we feel right now, even if it doesn't make sense, even if it seems completely irrational. Even though I might think I shouldn't feel this hateful, that's how I feel right now and I can't do anything about it.

It is appropriate to let ourselves feel these things and process them however we can. But at some point, we take a deep breath and sort through the feelings. We can take a step back and realize why we are feeling the way we do. We are angry because a loved one has been torn from us, and we feel guilty about that anger because we think we are hating the one we love.

Sometimes our postsuicide behavior is a mix of responses. If we find ourselves withdrawing from other people, it may be because we feel that our experience has set us apart from those still in the midst of "ordinary" life. Or we may withdraw out of an unconscious fear of abandonment; we don't want to get too close to others who may suddenly leave us as our loved one did. We distance ourselves from relationships because we don't want to open ourselves to future hurt. And so we resist well-meaning efforts of others who reach out to us.

We need to make a distinction between emotional feelings and behavioral responses. Nearly all of the emotions we feel are normal and to be expected. It is completely legitimate to feel anger, shame, guilt, sadness or despair. These emotions are primary responses to the suicide, and we simply experience them as they come.

On the other hand, we also have secondary behavioral responses that come after the primary emotions, and here is where we need to be careful. It can be entirely valid to be angry about the suicide, but we should not lash out and abuse our children. Our emotions are raw and real, but we can express them in ways that are not self-destructive or hurtful to others. If we need to release our anger, better to punch a pillow than a spouse. Yell out a window; don't throw a chair through it. Many survivors of suicide fall into alcohol or drug abuse in efforts to numb the pain and escape reality. Don't let this happen to you. Our grief feelings are normal, but not all responses to grief are healthy.

Traumatic bereavement may cause physical side effects, like a weakened immune system, proneness to illness, frequent headaches, loss of appetite, lack of energy and motivation and the like. This too is normal and usually goes away eventually. If symptoms have persisted long after your loved one's suicide, see your doctor and explain what you are struggling with.

While the turmoil of grief is excruciating in the moment, studies tell us that, for the most part, the emotional trauma is temporary. A long-term study of siblings of adolescent suicides found that "there appeared to be relatively few long-term adverse psychological consequences to the surviving children." Depression was common for the first six months following the death, and younger children were more affected than older ones. But adolescents were, on the whole, remarkably resilient, often reporting as adults that they "grew up quickly" or "matured more rapidly" following a sibling's suicide. Children of suicides, "although devastated and permanently marked by the suicide of a parent, for the most part survive the death without severe or enduring pathology."[31]

Likewise, the majority of surviving spouses adjust well in the long term. After an initial period of depression, most go on to bring up their children "with less difficulty than might be imagined. Less difficulty does not mean no difficulty, however, and the healing is exceedingly hard and takes a very long time."[32]

We never fully "recover" from a suicide; none of us will ever be the same. But while we are permanently changed, the emotional turmoil will not last forever. Scarred though we may be, we live on.

3

Lament

I lament all that might have been, and now will never be
NICHOLAS WOLTERSTORFF, ON THE DEATH OF
HIS TWENTY-FIVE-YEAR-OLD SON

I started to comprehend the enormity of my father's suicide when I went through some of his belongings. His watch and his glasses were sitting on the dresser. His wallet, with a picture of our family in it. His clarinet, which he had taught himself to play over the previous few years, had been silent since his stroke.

On his desk I found the last letter I had written to him and a boxed set of novels I had given him. One of them was missing, so he evidently had started to read it. Buried in the piles on his desk were books on Chinese healing and alternative medicine, which spoke of his desire to recover from his stroke and his attempts to rehabilitate himself.

As I went through Dad's things, I lamented a life that ended too soon, tomorrows that would not come, opportunities and occasions that would never be seen. Ellen and I had just married the previous year, and my father died before our first anniversary. Dad had not been able to visit us in Illinois, and he would never sign the little guestbook that we had received as a wedding present. He did not live to see our first child. These are all things that I lament.

I have rarely seen my brother cry, but one day shortly after Dad's death, Ed and I were talking. His eyes welled up with tears as he said, "Dad won't ever see me graduate from high school. He won't see me as a college student."

During my dad's depression, Mom had tried to give Dad things to look forward to. "Think of Ed getting married," she would say. "We will have grandchildren someday." Following the traditional Chinese emphasis on family, she tried to remind my father of the family members who looked to him. Someday others would be born who would want to know him. But my father was unable to cling to these hopes, and now my mother laments that they will not share their elderly years together.

When grieving a suicide we work through all sorts of regrets. We regret the *past*—mistakes made, arguments unresolved, all the things we wish we had said or done that are now impossible. We have regrets for the *present*—the immediacy of the loved one's absence, that he or she is no longer with us from day to day. We grieve the emptiness we feel at family gatherings and holiday meals. And we have regrets about the *future*—things that will now never take place.

Heather, a twenty-two-year-old recent college graduate at the time of her father's death, said, "When I first learned of my father's suicide, I cried because he would never walk me down the aisle at my wedding, and he would never know my future children. . . . I cried because we had so much unfinished business."[1]

Letting Ourselves Grieve

The grief process is a way of coming to terms with unfinished business. After moving through the initial shock and turmoil of a suicide, we usually come to a time when we fully enter into grief. This can be particularly difficult because life marches on, and we must return to our everyday routines. Even though we have been traumatically changed, we are expected to resume our responsibilities in the workplace, school, church and family. Our bereavement leave is over, and we are due back on the job. Just when life gets back to "normal," we may be grieving the most.

Christians sometimes think that we are not supposed to grieve, because our faith and theology provide us with confidence about heaven and eternal life. But while 1 Thessalonians 4:13 says that we are not to grieve as those without hope, we grieve nevertheless. Those without hope grieve in one way; those with hope grieve in another. Either way, grief is universal and not to be avoided. It is a legitimate response to loss.

Denying our grief can be hazardous. One pastor observes, "Mourning can turn some people soft and others hard."[2] We must be careful that our grief is constructive and not destructive, that it opens us up toward friends and family and does not embitter us toward life and others.

Our survival mechanism may be to stuff our feelings down inside us so they don't interfere with our daily duties. We may become stoic, keep a stiff upper lip and pretend that everything's fine. We may feel the need to be strong and not break down in tears. But this is not healthy.

As the eldest son, I initially felt a sense of responsibility to remain composed and in control, to provide some stability for my mother and other family members. But eventually I allowed myself to grieve more and cry more. Stephen Arterburn writes, "If Jesus can weep at the death of a friend, I think we can weep too."[3]

We must give ourselves permission to grieve. In fact, God expects that those who have experienced loss will grieve. Jesus taught, "Blessed are those who mourn, for they shall be comforted" (Matthew 5:4). This doesn't necessarily mean that we ought to be constantly in tears. Rather, it points to a simple truth: *Mourning is good.* When we mourn, we get outside what's going on inside. We grieve the emptiness, the tragedy of death, suicide, loss, the pain of the world. Only when we acknowledge the hurt can the hurt begin to heal.

This makes sense in the context of community as well. If we cover up our grief and try not to mourn, our pain will not be outwardly visible. It is then less likely that others will see our grief and comfort us. But if we do mourn and express outwardly our pain and grief, then friends and family will be aware of it and can respond with care and comfort. Only if we truly grieve can we be truly comforted.

In biblical times the Jewish people practiced certain rituals for mourning the death of a loved one. For seven days a family would stay home for intense grieving and to accept the condolences of neighbors. They would leave the house only to visit the tomb. Grievers would tear their garments and don sackcloth. They would put dust or ashes on their heads as public, visible signs of their loss. Then followed a thirty-day period of general mourning in which the family would not attend community events or leave town. Normal life resumed afterward, except in the case of a parent's death, in which the time of mourning would last for a year.[4]

Perhaps this can be instructive to us. We should be free to grieve visibly and publicly, with the expectation that those around us will give us space to grieve. While our communities today may not be quite as close-knit as those in the past, for the most part our colleagues and neighbors will understand if we need to take a break from some of our responsibilities in the aftermath of a death. A modern-day adaptation of early rituals of grieving might be for us to cut back on activities for a while. Maybe we hand over responsibility for teaching a Sunday school class to someone else for three or six months. Or we ask a coworker to cover for us on a particular project.

Counselors warn against two different extreme responses following a bereavement. Some people drown themselves in overactivity to hide from the pain of the loss. Others drop everything and retreat from the world. Neither is healthy; both are forms of distraction and escape from the reality of grief. Each of us must evaluate our own life, perhaps with the counsel of close friends and family, and decide what we think we can handle and what we should let go while in our first months of grief.

Having a period of mourning can also protect us from making mistakes. Those who lose a loved one to suicide should not make any major decisions or drastic changes in the first year of bereavement. Don't sell the house and move across the country. Don't remarry quickly to replace a missing spouse. Don't try to have another child as a substitute for the one you lost. While the length of time needed to grieve will vary from person to person, many give themselves a full year to explore the depth of their grief and to hold off from major life changes. The suicide is enough of a shock to the system; we don't need to complicate our lives with additional transitions. This moratorium on major choices can help us through a time when our decision-making abilities are hampered. If we are given a choice that seems questionable, we can remind ourselves, *No, I won't do that—I am in my time of mourning.*

Fully entering into a period of true mourning will help us grow past denial. Denial might be okay as a temporary phase, as a coping mechanism to get through some of the hardest parts. But we should not become numb and deaden our emotions. "Because grief is so painful, some people try to 'get over' a loss by denying the pain. Studies show that when people don't deal with the emotions of grief, the pain does not go away. It remains with them, and can turn up in unrecognizable and sometimes destructive ways."[5] We must allow ourselves to feel the grief and loss, because only when we actively mourn will we be able to receive the comfort that God and others offer.

Bob lost two loved ones to suicide within the span of fifteen months—his brother-in-law, Chris, and his best friend, Bill. Though he wanted to flee from the grief and pain, he said that "the only way out of this grief is through it—not around, under, over, or retreating from it. I must let the deep pain hurt. I must sorrow. I must question. I must cry. I must unload on friends and not keep this bottled up in me."[6]

Grief cannot be resolved by avoiding it. It must be faced. Gerald

Sittser found a helpful image: "The quickest way for anyone to reach the sun and the light of day is not to run west, chasing after the setting sun, but to head east, plunging into the darkness until one comes to the sunrise."[7]

The Practice of Lament

My soul is in anguish.
How long, O LORD, how long? . .

I am worn out from groaning;
all night long I flood my bed with weeping
and drench my couch with tears. (Psalm 6:3, 6)

Lament is not a word we commonly use to describe our grief, but it points to an ancient tradition. While we normally understand grief as an *emotion* that we *feel*, lament is an *activity* that we *practice*.

Lament is a way of articulating and making sense of grief. In Old Testament times, mourners often composed psalms of lament in which they poured out their heartache, pain and rage to God. In these songs they declared to God and those around them that all was not well in the world, that they were in the midst of unimaginable anguish.

The book of Lamentations is a structured form of lament: five acrostic poems exploring grief and agony. This exemplifies lament as "ordered grief," giving grief a particular shape and form. Likewise in the laments in the book of Psalms, grieving, hurting people used a particular poetic structure to make their sorrow and complaints known to God.[8] These psalms move through a variety of expressions of grief, usually starting with a cry to God and a description of the situation, then offering a prayer for God's response, with a conclusion expressing hope and confidence that God has heard and will answer the appeal.

Biblical scholar Walter Brueggemann writes, "Israel knew how to order its grief, not only to get that grief fully uttered and delivered but also to be sure that, said in its fullness untameable, it is not turned loose with destructiveness."[9] In lament our raw emotions are ordered, disciplined and transformed. They are given form and expression so that our hurt and loss become more understandable and accessible.

This can be helpful when we find ourselves lost in the nebulousness of grief. "Grief itself, by its very nature, is a rather formless thing. The mind of a person in deep sorrow characteristically moves in circles, returning again and again to the source of the grief, unable to leave it and unable to resolve it."[10] Counselors talk about the need to process feelings and emotions after a tragedy. The ancients did this through the practice of lament. We can move through our emotions in lament, perhaps through journaling or writing letters or poetry.

Lament also focuses our grief in the proper direction—it turns us toward God. After a suicide, it is natural for us to shake a fist at the heavens and ask, "God, how could you let this happen?" Sometimes we think we ought not have such outbursts, but the book of Psalms reminds us that we are free to bring all our emotions before God, however volatile or intense they may be. One helpful practice is to read some relevant psalms and paraphrase them for our situation. We may identify phrases that particularly resonate with us, and we can personalize the psalms as our own prayers to God.

For example, Eugene Peterson's *The Message* paraphrase of Psalm 130 says: "Help, God—the bottom has fallen out of my life! Master, hear my cry for help!" Those of us who have lost a loved one to suicide can easily pray this prayer.

Lament is not passive acceptance. We do not merely resign ourselves to the cruelties of life. Instead we declare that this is not the way it's supposed to be. We rage against the messed-up world that drives people to despair. Lament grieves. It mourns that this is the way things are, that they are not the way God intended.

But while lament can be cathartic, we should not have a naive expectation that the expression of our lament will quickly resolve our grief. "When we lament, we acknowledge the truth that God does not remove all the pain and torment of dying, either for the sufferer or for the community."[11]

Retelling the Story

Nature writer and suicide hotline volunteer Diane Ackerman describes one counselor's experience:

> One Sunday morning in 1971, Lewis was summoned to a terrifying scene. A man was holding a loaded gun on his family, threatening to kill them and himself and anyone else who got in the way. Lewis walked right into the man's house, sat down beside him, and said quietly: "Tell me your story." Ten hours later, the man gave him the gun.

Somehow listening to someone's life story has the power to save life. Ackerman concludes that the truth revealed in this event is that "each of us has a story, each of us has a loaded gun that we aim at ourselves. After hours, or years, of talking, the story can at last be told in its fullness, and the gun can be laid down."[12]

Morbid though it may seem, retelling the story of our loved one's death can help us through our loss. In some strange way, it sustains us. After watching her twentysomething son jump to his death from a fourteenth-story terrace, one mother said, "What I wanted was to talk and talk, go over it again and again, and that kept me alive in some strange way I still don't understand."[13]

Telling the story is a form of lament, of ordering our grief. It helps us process the events and move beyond denial. When we tell the story, whether speaking out loud or writing on paper, we confront ourselves with the reality of the suicide. We may say to others, "I can't believe this is happening, but here's what happened." Doing so helps us come to grips with the fact that our loved one *is* gone. Telling the story prevents us from escaping into a fantasy world where nothing happened and everything is fine.

Furthermore, telling the story helps others understand what we have experienced and how we are feeling. It gives them the opportunity to listen to us and share our grief. If possible, survivors should find a trusted individual, perhaps a family member, pastor, counselor, chaplain or friend, with whom they can share their stories. Kathleen Norris says all pastors know that "listening is often the major part of ministry, that people in a crisis need to tell their story, from beginning to end, and the best thing—often the only thing—that you can do is to sit there and take it in."[14]

This is why it is often helpful to attend a support group for suicide survivors. This is a safe place where survivors invite one another, "Tell me your story." Even if at first you cannot bring yourself to share your own story, it can be helpful just to sit and listen to other people tell theirs. Hearing each other's stories can be comforting. As difficult as it may be, hearing about someone else's experience with the suicide of a loved one gives us a point of connection. It shows us that we are not alone, that someone else can identify with our loss.

Furthermore, entering into other people's stories of loss enables us to enter into their stories of healing. The fact that they are living and breathing to tell us their experience gives us hope that we too can survive and heal.

Telling the Truth

In his memoir *Telling Secrets* novelist Frederick Buechner tells the story of his father's suicide. Buechner was only ten years old when his father went into the garage and ran the Chevy until the exhaust fumes killed him. There was no funeral to mark his death, and afterward Buechner's family avoided the subject. His father had hoped that no one would find out that he had taken his own life, but friends and family members did realize what had happened.

"His suicide was a secret we nonetheless tried to keep as best we could," Buechner writes, "and after a while my father himself became such a secret." The unintended consequence of avoiding the reality of his suicide was to negate his very existence. "By not speaking of what we remembered about him we soon simply stopped remembering at all. . . . In almost no time at all, it was as if, at least for me, he had never existed."[15]

We cannot fully lament a death if we do not acknowledge its reality. After we have experienced initial shock and denial, we must

come to the place where we face it squarely. We cannot deceive ourselves that it was not a suicide. Though it may be tempting to resort
to euphemisms about the death, we must tell the truth to ourselves
and others. If we hide from the suicide and go on with our lives pre-
tending that it never occurred, we may inadvertently dishonor the
memory of our loved one. If we avoid reckoning with the death, we
can create a mental block that makes it harder for us to remember the
person's life as well. We may grow so accustomed to never thinking
or speaking of the suicide that we end up not acknowledging that the
person ever existed at all.

"The awkwardness of grief tempts us to hide from the truth,"
writes pastor Randy Christian. "Those bereaved by suicide are
tempted to avoid the painful fact that a loved one took his or her life.
But hiding from that fact only makes it harder to recover from the
grief."[16] If we are truly to lament and grieve our loved one's death,
we must be honest about the suicide.

Christian tells the story of Clara, a young woman whose husband
died in a tragic "accident." Because they lived in a small town, she
wanted to suppress gossip and rumors about her husband's death.
The coroner, a family friend, tried to ease Clara's pain by ruling the
death accidental. The truth emerged years later when her son was old
enough to ask questions about his father's death, and the cumulative
effect of years of self-deception was emotional damage. "Clara's
friends had done her no favor by helping her hide from the truth,"
writes Christian.[17]

Many of us come from family systems in which certain topics were
taboo. Perhaps we never talked about our mother's alcoholism or our
father's abusiveness. Maybe at family reunions conversation steered
clear of an aunt's divorce or a wayward teen's rebellion. We grew up
learning unspoken rules about which topics were allowed and which
were forbidden. We simply avoided certain areas because to bring
them up would bring shame upon the family. These subtle "can't
talk" rules are usually intended to protect the family from hurt or ridi-
cule, but they also prevent healthy reckoning with hard realities.

These lies hold us hostage to denial, whereas the truth sets us free to grieve and heal.

After my father's suicide, I began to probe some of the darker areas of my family's history. I learned from my mother that my family has some history of mental illness. My father's mother became schizophrenic when he was five or six years old. This was in rural Taiwan right after World War II, a place and an era in which no one really knew how to deal with mental disorders. My grandmother was institutionalized in an asylum for the mentally ill for about ten years and died there when my father was a teenager. "Your dad never, ever talked about it," my mom told me. "He kept it inside him all the time."

My mom also told me about another relative whose college girlfriend had died by suicide. The family never talked about her either. I asked my mother if it was okay that I was asking about all this. "I'm glad you can talk about it," she replied. "Your dad could never talk about things, how he was feeling. But you can talk about it, get it out. That's healthier."

Sometimes we avoid telling the truth about our loved one's suicide because we think we are protecting others from realities that are too harsh. This is especially true when young children are survivors—grandchildren, children or siblings of the suicide. Parents may believe they are protecting the children by offering less disturbing explanations, like "Daddy was in an accident." But counselors tell us that "protecting" children from the truth doesn't work, because the truth will inevitably come out.

One man was told as a child that his father's overdose was accidental. Decades later he asked his mother what had really happened, and she admitted that the death had been a suicide. In cases like this, not only do the adult children have to reckon with the shock and grief of the newly discovered suicide, but they also have to grapple with the fact that the truth was withheld from them for all those years. They may feel betrayed.

"Protecting" a child by hiding the truth only leads to deception.

The surviving parent or guardian will steer clear of talking about the suicide, and this prevents healthy communication with the child. Other family members may get drawn in, required to observe the "can't talk" rule. However, the truth will eventually emerge, because people outside the family will not know that the children are not "supposed" to know the facts of the death. Something inevitably slips in a conversation, and then the children realize that they have been misled about their relative's death. Better that they learn the truth sooner, from a trusted parent or adult who can communicate the reality gently and carefully.

The challenge is finding age-appropriate ways to tell the truth to children. It is not helpful to use euphemisms, because they lead to further hurt. If we say, "Daddy went on a long trip," the child will fear that any trip will lead to abandonment. If we say, "Your sister went to sleep," the child will be fearful of bedtime as a doorway to death. Saying "God took him home to heaven" will lead children to blame God for the suicide.[18] Counselors Ann Smolin and John Guinan write,

> When the child asks, "How did my mommy die?" he needs to be told as simply, directly, and truthfully as possible. Even if he does not fully understand what you tell him at this time, you are laying the groundwork for fuller comprehension as he grows older and more able to understand what has been said to him. One way to proceed is to tell him that mommy had a sickness that made her so sad that she did not wish to live anymore. . . . Tell him that you know there are lots of ways to deal with bad problems and you are very sorry that mommy chose this way, which is not a good way. She chose a forever way, so she will never know that she could have found another way to deal with her terrible sadness.[19]

Likewise, a social worker whose psychiatrist husband killed himself told her children, "He had a sickness that was like a cancer which could not be cured."[20] These kinds of explanations can be sensitive and truthful at the same time.

The reality of lament is that it may take some time, perhaps even years or decades, to break the silence and fully tell the truth about a suicide. Buechner avoided telling the secrets of his father's death until some forty years afterward. He came to a place where he was able to imagine a dialogue with his father, through which he was able to rediscover childhood feelings he had nearly forgotten. He eventually wrote a novel, *The Wizard's Tide*, a fictionalized version of his father's suicide, except with one key difference: the young protagonist is able to talk to his sister about what happened to their father. "It was enough to start a healing process for the children in the story that for me didn't start until I was well into my fifties," Buechner writes. "Stranger still, it was enough also to start healing the child in me the way he might have been healed in 1936 if his real story had only turned out like the make-believe story in the book."[21]

True lament means that we tell the truth about our loved one's suicide, both to others and to ourselves. Telling our secrets opens the door to healing.

Lament as Love Song

After his son's death in a mountain-climbing accident, philosopher Nicholas Wolterstorff told the story of his grief in a short book called *Lament for a Son*. He was practicing the discipline of lament. He was getting his grief out on paper, wrestling with his questions and also honoring his son's life.

Ten years later Wolterstorff learned that a friend had given copies of the book to all of his children. "Why did you do that?" he asked.

"Because it is a love-song," his friend replied.

Wolterstorff was taken aback, but he realized, "Yes, it is a love-song. Every lament is a love-song."[22]

We lament because we love. We call those we have lost our "loved ones." If we did not love them, we would not lament them. Our grief is birthed out of our love, care and concern for those who have left us. Our grief is a sign of our love.

"Love in our world is suffering love," Wolterstorff writes. "Some do not suffer much, though, for they do not love much. Suffering is for the loving. If I hadn't loved him, there wouldn't be this agony."[23]

As we lament, whatever form that may take, we are rememberi

our loved ones and expressing our love. "Particularly in the case of premature or tragic deaths, it is appropriate for Christians to adopt or develop rituals and liturgies of lament to remember those who died."[24] Painful though this may be, our love for those who are gone will carry us through the grief.

The stage play and movie *Shadowlands,* based on the life and marriage of C. S. Lewis and Joy Gresham, accentuates this connection between love and pain. In the course of their relationship, Gresham is struck by cancer and her death is imminent. Lewis wishes she didn't have to suffer the pain, but she rebukes him, saying that the pain is part of the happiness. If we did not experience pain, we would not experience love either. After Lewis's wife has died, he acknowledges that the grief and pain he now experiences are part of the happiness and love he had with her in life.

Paradoxically, in our grief we understand the magnitude of our love. The cliché says that we don't know what we have until it's gone, but the truth is that the grief we feel in our loved one's absence is an indication of the love we had for them while they were present with us. The agony we undergo is the score on which our love ballad is written.

4

Relinquishment

Dear Lord, bring me through darkness into light.
Bring me through pain into peace. Bring me through death
into life. Be with me wherever I go, and with everyone I love.
In Christ's name I ask it. Amen.

A PRAYER WRITTEN FOR FREDERICK BUECHNER'S
DYING BROTHER

The day before my father's funeral, we had a private family visitation at the funeral home. We went into the chapel to view Dad's body, lying in the casket, dressed up in the new suit he had bought the previous year for my wedding.

Mom started to cry, and my brother and I slipped away so she could have some time alone with him. I lingered at the back of the room while she talked to him. She was talking in Chinese, and I couldn't hear or understand what she was saying. It sounded as if she had a lot of things she wanted to say. Questions, perhaps, but no answers. They had been married nearly three decades.

I too spent some time alone with Dad. I stood in front of the casket for a while and then reached in and touched his hand. He felt cold and waxy, and it was odd to think that this same man had held me as a child and played tennis with me as a youth. I didn't see the signs of strangulation around his neck; the undertaker had cleaned that up. I saw a few marks at the back of his head from the autopsy, but apart from that he looked much as he had in life.

I told him I was glad that we had gotten along better in the last few years, that we had been able to tell each other, "I love you." I said thanks for all the ways he had provided for me, and I thanked him for coming to my graduations and my wedding. I told him I'd make sure Mom and Ed were okay, and I said I hoped to see him again someday.

Only once before had I seen someone in a casket, back in elementary school when a classmate had died of cancer. I had gotten in trouble for talking during the funeral. Back then I didn't understand the finality of death. Three of my grandparents had died by the time of my father's death, but I had not gone to any of their funerals because they had been out of the country. So my father's death was my first up-close encounter with the enormity of death. It was the first time I had come face to face with a loved one who had died.

Suddenly death was real, in all of its awful finality. This visitation and the funeral and burial to come were my chances to say goodbye to my father. He was gone, and he wasn't coming back.

Approaching Death

Suicide is usually so jarring to survivors that the death doesn't seem real. We imagine that it is only a dream, that the loved one is not actually dead. But at some point it sinks in, and we relinquish ourselves to the reality of death. But is death something that we should accept with resignation, rage against or welcome? Christians have looked at death from a variety of angles, and some of their reflections can help us come to grips with it.

As spiritual writer Henri Nouwen approached his sixties, he had a greater awareness of his own mortality, and he spent five weeks in solitude, meditating, thinking and writing about death. During that time he realized that he was unprepared to die. So he set about reconciling himself to a death that would come sooner or later.

Considering what it means to die well, Nouwen concludes that "a good death is a death in solidarity with others." If we see death as an event that separates us from others, then it will be sad and sorrowful. Nouwen raises another possibility. Because all of us will experience death someday, we participate in a universal human experience. "Death can become a celebration of our unity with the human race," he writes. "Instead of separating us from others, death can unite us with others; instead of being sorrowful, it can give rise to new joy; instead of simply ending life, it can begin something new."[1]

All of us have seen media images of tragedies around the world: civil wars, famines, earthquakes, terrorist attacks. All over the globe people die suddenly and abruptly. In every nation and every culture, people grieve the deaths of loved ones. Because we share in this human experience, we understand their pain and loss. I have found myself grieving the deaths of people I have never met and will never know, whose deaths are only mentioned briefly on the news. In some small way I have come to identify with this universal human experience.

Nouwen notes that Jesus anticipated his own death. His words in John 16 show that Jesus knew his death was approaching, and he wanted his disciples to be ready for it. Nouwen writes, "We *can choose* to befriend our death as Jesus did. We *can choose* to live as God's beloved children in solidarity with all people, trusting in our ultimate fruitfulness. And in so doing, we can also become people who care for others. As men and women who have faced our mortality, we can help our brothers and sisters to dispel the darkness of death and guide them to the light of God's grace."[2]

Death as Friend
Henri Nouwen was a good friend of Joseph Cardinal Bernardin, the former archbishop of Chicago. In 1995 Nouwen gave Bernardin a copy of his book *Our Greatest Gift*, as Bernardin had been undergoing treatment for cancer and was meditating on his imminent death.

Bernardin later wrote, "The main thing I remember is that he talked about the importance of looking on death as a friend rather than an enemy. While I had always taken such a view in terms of my faith, I needed to be reminded at that moment because I was rather exhausted from the radiation treatment." Bernardin recalled that Nouwen said, "People of faith, who believe that death is the transition from this life to life eternal, should see it as a friend."[3]

Nouwen suddenly died of a heart attack on September 21, 1996, at age fifty-nine. A few months afterward, on November 14, Bernardin died from pancreatic cancer. I remember watching coverage of his funeral and memorial services on TV, as all of Chicago mourned the archbishop. People from all religious backgrounds and walks of life testified that Bernardin's example had given them hope and inspiration.

Bernardin's last book, *The Gift of Peace,* was published a few months after his death. In it he reflects on the process he underwent. As it became clear that the cancer had returned and would bring his earthly life to an end, he decided that he would not fight against death. He instead would see it as a friend and the doorway to eternal life. Death is a threshold that we all must cross, he says, and for those who live in hope of eternal life with God, it is not to be feared but to be welcomed.

Bernardin addresses his readers thus: "I invite those who read this book to walk with me the final miles of my life's journey. When we reach the gate, I will have to go in first—that seems to be the rule: one at a time by designation. But know that I will carry each of you in my heart! Ultimately, we will all be together, intimately united with the Lord Jesus whom we love so much."[4] His book ends with a famous prayer of St. Francis of Assisi:

> O Divine Master, grant that I may not so much seek
> to be consoled, as to console;
> to be understood, as to understand;
> to be loved, as to love;
> for it is in giving that we receive,
> it is in pardoning that we are pardoned.
> It is in dying that we are born to eternal life.

Death as Intruder

I am grateful for the profound wisdom of Nouwen and Bernardin. They have contemplated death and understood it far more deeply than I ever will. And yet something in me recoils from their meditations. They seem too nice, too affirming of death, too optimistic about death's benefits. It is one thing when someone has the luxury of approaching death gradually, in old age or illness. It is another thing entirely when a loved one is ripped from this life by his or her own hand.

For that reason, death seems to me an intruder. When suicide strikes, death does not feel like a friend. It feels like a terrorist who has cut down an innocent bystander. And a suicide death feels like the worst trickery: death has enticed someone into willingly entering into it. In the case of suicide, death is a deceiver, a manipulator, the worst of adversaries.

Death is like the evil queen who gave Snow White a poisoned apple. Death dangled something that looked good in front of our loved ones; it whispered to them that death would mean relief, freedom, escape. Death poisoned them with this thinking. It seduced them into believing a lie.

Death has lied to our loved ones and persuaded them that they should embrace it. We who are left behind wish we could have convinced them otherwise. We want the chance to retaliate against death, to refute the lie that death is better than life. We are violated by death. In the case of suicide, death is not a friend. It is an enemy.

Death as Enemy

We may be tempted to relinquish ourselves to the normality of loss. We might resign ourselves to seeing death just as part of the human experience.[5] But the notion that death is normal and expected comes more from modern psychology than from biblical teaching. "Death is primarily, according to the biblical accounts, neither 'a part of life' nor the 'last stage of growth,' but a terrible disruption of the life God's people live with God and, as such, a subject of fear, loathing, and pain."[6]

Death is not to be passively accepted. It may be a "normal" part of life, but it is still an enemy to be battled and overcome. "Death is sha-lom's mortal enemy. Death is demonic. We cannot live at peace with death."[7]

One of the clearest biblical images of death is found in the New Testament. The apostle Paul declares in his first letter to the Corin-thians that death is an enemy. Paul says that God will put all his ene-mies under Christ's feet. And "the last enemy to be destroyed is death" (1 Corinthians 15:26).

So the Bible sees death as an enemy. Though death is a universal human experience, we should not then assume that it is a *natural* human experience. It is not what God intended. It is a result of the Fall, of things being corrupted from the way they were meant to be. Death is a violation of God's original plan for his people. Death is an enemy because it runs counter to life.

God is life. He is the source of life, and all that is good is found in him. All that lives comes from the life-giving Spirit of God. Death is the enemy of life because it disrupts the life that God intended.

Yet death is not the end. God has decisively acted in history to defeat death. In the person of Jesus of Nazareth, God challenged the powers of death. Death lay hold of God himself. Death crucified Jesus, the One who called himself the Bread of Life. But death could not hold Jesus in the grave. God raised Jesus from his tomb, declaring to all humanity that the power of death has been broken. Now humanity can be assured that life will prevail.

Jesus himself had walked through death and come out on the other side. Life triumphed over death. Death is no longer the end. As theologian Alister McGrath writes,

> The cross liberates us from this malignant tyranny of death. It breaks its oppressive stranglehold over us. . . . It is true that in the midst of life, we are in death. But it is even more true that in the midst of death, we are in life—the eternal life made available to us through the gospel, which nothing—not even death itself—can take away from us.[8]

God has indeed conquered death. Nicholas Wolterstorff points out that "when the writer of Revelation spoke of the coming of the day of shalom, he did not say that on that day we would live at peace with death."[9] Rather, on that day "there will be no more death or mourning or crying or pain, for the old order of things has passed away" (Revelation 21:4). In the world to come there is no place for death.

So while we live on this earth, death is expected but has lost its sting. It is a defeated enemy because it cannot ultimately hold power over us and separate us from God. "Death remains an evil, but it no longer has the capacity to sever the communion of God's people with their Lord."[10] As Paul writes in Romans 8, neither life *nor death* can separate us from the love of God in Christ.

Bernardin and Nouwen are correct that death can be befriended when seen in light of God's ultimate victory over death. We can do so not because death is an inherent good but because it is no longer the ultimate threat that will end our existence and life. Jesus has seen to that. As the author of the book of Hebrews writes, by his death Jesus defeated the power of death and freed "those who all their lives were held in slavery by their fear of death" (Hebrews 2:15). Death has been declawed, neutered. Death is the ultimate and final enemy, but an enemy to be feared no longer, for it is defeated.

What does this mean for us? It means that while we relinquish ourselves to the reality of our loved one's death, we know that death does not have the final word. In the end, death itself will die.

Yearning for Shalom
In Jewish and Christian tradition, the word *shalom* is used to describe the way things are supposed to be. It is often translated as "peace," but shalom is far more than the absence of war or conflict. Shalom has a sense of fulfillment and completeness. "Shalom means *universal flourishing, wholeness, and delight*—a rich state of affairs in which natural needs are satisfied and natural gifts fruitfully employed, a state of affairs that inspires joyful wonder as its Creator and Savior opens doors and welcomes the creatures in whom he delights. Shalom, in other words, is the way things ought to be."[11]

We live in a fallen, imperfect world where things are not the way they ought to be. Wars rage, diseases afflict people, societies are plagued with poverty and racism, and we lose loved ones to suicide. The world is filled with death. This is not the way it was supposed to be. This is a world yearning for healing and the restoration of shalom.

In our grief, we long for peace. We are desperate for rest from the drain of conflicting emotions. Not only do we dream of the cessation of the pain and agony, we also yearn for the return of something approaching normalcy—for shalom. We want shelter from the storm of trauma. We look for hope and life when we are surrounded by despair and death. So I find hope in an episode from the life of Jesus, in which he and his friends traveled across the Sea of Galilee in a small boat. Imagine what it might have been like.

The sky is clear and blue. You smell the surf in the air; you hear seagulls crying in the distance, you feel the breeze at your back and the gentle roll of the boat on the waters.

But wait. Dark clouds appear in the distance, looming ominously over the horizon. Without warning, the wind picks up. The temperature drops; there's a chill in the air. You feel a raindrop, then another. In no time the sky is black. A flash of lightning crackles overhead. You hear the boom of thunder. The clouds open up, and sheets of rain come driving down upon you, stinging your skin.

The water churns and becomes a tempest, and the boat careens up and down on the waves. Ten-foot breakers crash over the side of the boat, threatening to swamp you. You grab the mast and hold on for dear life. You think you're going to be sick.

"Shore!" someone yells. "We've got to get back to shore!" But it's too late. You're too far out. The rain is coming down so hard you can't even see the shoreline.

Your panic is rising. You're a fisherman, you do this for a living, but this is no ordinary storm. The sail is torn to shreds; you try to pull it together, but it's beyond your control. You can't even hear each other screaming over the wind. There's nothing you can do. Perhaps this is the storm that's going to sink you once and for all.

Then you realize Jesus is sound asleep! He's just lying there, taking a nap in the stern of the boat. How can he sleep in a storm like this? You stagger across the boat, grab him by the shoulder and shake him, yelling, "Teacher! Teacher! Wake up! Save us! We're going to die! Don't you care if we drown?"

Jesus stands. He looks at you and your terrified companions. He turns his head and surveys the storm around him. Then he raises his arm to the whirling waves and cries out, "Peace! Be still!"

Instantly the wind drops from typhoon to nothing. Absolutely nothing. The storm vanishes. The sky is blue and cloudless. The water is calm and smooth. The sudden silence is deafening.

"Oh, you of little faith," Jesus whispers. "Why were you so afraid?"

You sit back in the boat, dripping wet, gasping to catch your breath. You can hear your heart pounding. All you can do is wonder, Who is this man? Even the winds and the waves obey him!

On one level this narrative gives us hope for surviving the storm of suicide. As survivors of trauma, we may feel as if we are in a storm where our boat is about to capsize. We may feel we are about to perish, the storms of life are going to sink us forever. After all, the storms are bigger than us, and we can't save ourselves. But in the Christian faith, God provides shelter from the storms. Though the storms are bigger than we are, God is bigger than the storms. He does not sleep in ignorance of our plight. If we call out to him, he will answer. He is the One who says, "Peace! Be still!" to the storms of life. In the midst of our turmoil, he grants us peace.

However, there's another layer of significance to this passage. This is not merely a miracle story that shows God's power over the elements. More significantly, the Gospel writers deliberately use language and word choices that foreshadow Jesus' death and resurrection.[12] In the stilling of the storm Jesus *rises* out of *slumber* to *save* the disciples from *perishing*. This is intentional imagery to evoke the resurrection. Jesus was asleep in death, and he arose to save us from perishing and to give us new life.

This story is a microcosm of the gospel message. In effect, it shows us that God is not merely a God who calms the storms in our lives. After all, he does not immediately calm every crisis we encounter, and we might thus conclude that he is a minor deity incapable or unwilling to help us. This is not the case at all. More important, he is the Creator and Redeemer God who has calmed the ultimate storm of death. On that basis we can trust him to take care of us in the midst of life's storms.

God does not only address the storms—he also addresses us. "Shalom," he says. "Peace, be still." Be still and know that God is there. He goes through the storms with us. He is the God who has conquered death. He rises to save us from perishing. He will restore shalom and bring things back to the way they are supposed to be.

5

Remembrance

Unless we remember we cannot understand.
EDWARD M. FORSTER

After any death, we find ourselves surrounded by reminders of the loved one's life: the vacant bedroom, the abandoned toothbrush, the shoes in the front closet, the empty place at the table. I studied the things my father left behind. The baseball cap he wore in the summers when he mowed the lawn. The blue sweater I had always liked.

I pulled his Ph.D. dissertation off his bookshelf. Though I had looked at it before, I had never noticed the acknowledgments, which ended, "Finally, I would like to thank my wife, Emily, for her invaluable help and understanding, and my son, Albert, for being patient during this period of my study and preparation of this work." I was three years old when he finished his doctorate.

I also remembered the things he had given me over the years: a watch when I was in eighth grade, a wallet for my fifteenth birthday, a new watch when I finished graduate school. I still use them all, and often when I look at the time or pull out my wallet, I think of Dad.

At first these reminders can be painful, triggering deep grief all over again. But eventually they are transformed from reminders of a loved one's death to remembrances of his or her life. Rather than talismans that remind us of their absence, they become opportunities to affirm their meaning and significance to us.

The Funeral of a Suicide

Funerals help us come to terms with the reality of a person's death as well as serving as a time of remembrance of his or her life. Difficult enough under "ordinary" circumstances, funerals for suicides can be tremendously heartrending unless handled with sensitivity and grace. One church denomination recommends,

> When a suicide does occur, congregations and pastors minister to the bereaved and deceased through Christian burial and their loving support. Funerals are not occasions either to condemn or idealize an act of suicide, but times to proclaim that suicide and death itself do not place one beyond the communion of saints. Because of Christ's death and resurrection for us, we entrust a troubled person to God's love and mercy with the promise that "whether we live or whether we die, we are the Lord's" (Romans 14:7).[1]

Doug, a pastor, had an uncle who had also been a pastor and missionary. For reasons unknown, his uncle took his own life. Doug participated in the funeral service, and his message focused on "reminding those who had gathered that the impact of my uncle's life was to be measured by his years of devotion to Christ, not by how his life had ended. My intention was not to minimize the tragedy of suicide. That decision has left some deep scars in the lives of those left behind, but it is not the full story of a man's life either."[2]

My brother's youth pastor, Scott, officiated at my father's funeral. He met with our family beforehand to get a better sense of what my dad had been like and to talk about the service. Scott asked how we wanted to handle the fact of the suicide, admitting that he had never performed a funeral for a suicide and wasn't quite sure what to say. We agreed that it would be best to be straightforward and gave him permission to explain the circumstances of Dad's death.

I happened to have a book about funeral sermons, and it included a section on what to say for a suicide. It quoted a sermon for a young man who had shot himself: "Our friend died on his own battlefield. He was killed in action fighting a civil war."[3] I lent the book to Scott, thinking he might find it helpful in his preparations.

The funeral program included a short biography of my father, mentioning such accomplishments as being one of the top five students in a national college entrance exam in Taiwan, as well as describing his personality traits and family life. Here is how we handled the cause of his death:

> Terry suffered a stroke on November 21, 1997. His left hand and foot became debilitated. After some therapeutic treatments, he slowly recuperated and was able to walk and move his hand. But as a side effect from the stroke, a severe clinical depression took a hold of him. This eventually became so critical that despite a month of treatment for the illness, he was no longer able to go on living.
>
> In the months prior to his death, Terry came to recognize the frailty and limitations of the physical body. He began to seek God, to read the Bible and to pray. He told God he was sorry for all the things he had done wrong in his life, and he asked Jesus to forgive him of his sins and to be his Savior. Though he is no longer with us, it is our hope that his spirit is at rest with the Lord.

Several family members and friends delivered eulogies. I recounted how, when I was in Cub Scouts in first grade, I asked my dad to help me make a pinewood derby racecar. He brought his engineering expertise to bear on the project and essentially designed and constructed the car by himself. All I did was paint it. It won first place that year.

Just before the message, Ellen sang the hymn "It Is Well with My Soul" with my accompaniment on the piano. Scott explained that this song was born out of loss, that Horatio Spafford had lost his daughters at sea and had written this hymn while traveling by sea in the area where his children had died. He then read a quotation, "We just keep losing things."[4] This is the opening line of a book published by my company; this fact provided me an odd sort of comfort in the midst of the funeral.

I wondered how Scott would handle the fact of the suicide. He took his cue from the book I had loaned him, saying,

> Answers never come easy after a death, particularly when the death resulted from the person taking their own life. Depression was the enemy Terry battled against after he suffered his stroke in November. He fought an enemy that was as real to him as this casket is to us. This silent enemy exhausted all his courage and strength. Only God knows what he was suffering in his soul. For those who saw Terry's struggle, you wonder what you could have done differently. To receive the comfort God offers we need to resist the regrets and the "only if I would haves." We want to resist the regret and realize that Terry's life should not be measured by how it tragically ended, but in how it was lived.

He went on to offer both comfort and hope, reminding us that God is "the Father of compassion and the God of all comfort" (2 Corinthians 1:3). At the committal service, Scott read Psalm 139 and concluded by saying, "We commit the body of Terry to the ground; his spirit we leave in the hands of a merciful God. May the living learn the lessons this day and experience the comfort of Jesus Christ, who said, 'I am the resurrection and the life. He who believes in me will live, even though he dies; and whoever lives and believes in me will never die.'"

The Gifts of Memory

Funerals, memorial services, wakes and receptions are all opportunities to remember and commemorate a loved one's life. I learned quite a bit about my dad that week that I had never quite understood. For example, in 1984 my dad was awarded his company's Technical Excellence Award. He received a large bronze plaque that we hung on the family room wall. I never knew what it was for. I simply assumed that he had received the award for doing good work, whatever that might have been.

I included the Technical Excellence Award in my dad's biography in the program, and at the funeral one of Dad's coworkers said that he was glad to see it had been mentioned. He explained that the company had been working on a large project with many different computer components and all sorts of technical specifications. Many problems needed constant correction. But the system that my dad had designed was perfect. It worked flawlessly, "out of the box" as they say, and had needed no debugging or changes at all.

I had never really known what my dad did in his work. He was an electrical engineer, and I figured he designed mainframes or other computer systems for corporations. I also knew that his division did some work for the government. But he never talked about what he did from day to day. I had always assumed that it was because he was from a generation that compartmentalized different spheres of life—work was work, home was home, and you never talked about one in the other.

I was wrong. At the funeral I learned that my dad never talked about his work because he *couldn't*—he had a top-level security clearance that prevented him from talking about the projects he worked on, even with his wife and children. He could discuss them only with people who had the same level of clearance. Some of those people were at the funeral and reception, and they told me that my dad's work with computer image processing had helped the United States win the Persian Gulf War. He had designed devices that allowed orbiting satellites to identify buildings and pinpoint an individual or object's location. That kind of intelligence helped give the United States the upper hand over Iraq.

Immigrants like my father were not usually given clearance to work on government contracts, but the company had made an exception for my dad. In fact, he was the only foreign-born employee granted such high clearance levels. Evidently he was not supposed to talk with anyone who could leak information back to a foreign country, so he limited his contacts with Taiwanese and Chinese friends.

I also learned more about my dad as a worker and a person. One of his subordinates told me that when people were discussing a problem in staff meetings, if my dad spoke up and made suggestions, everybody deferred to him. When a coworker heard of his death, he said, "This company is done for!" because nobody else had his kind of technical genius. His coworkers told me that he had always been well respected, kind and modest, the third-highest-ranking person in his division. He was seen as a mentor, an innovator, an expert in his field.

His colleagues also told me that he was proud of his sons. That meant a lot to me, to hear that he said so to others. I had had a rocky relationship with my father over the years, so I was deeply grateful for the stories they told and the things I learned about my father that week. Despite the grief and pain, each person's remembrance was a gift I could take with me.

The Importance of Remembrance

While visiting the cemetery some months after my father's death, I thought about the significance of having a headstone to identify a gravesite. Without it, we could not find someone's resting place. As sad as it may be to remember the death of a loved one, it is even more tragic when people die with no one to remember them. I thought of the victims of war and genocide, buried anonymously in mass graves in Bosnia or Rwanda. These people do not even have markers to identify them, families to grieve them. They have disappeared into the recesses of history, never to be recovered. It is almost as if they had never lived. They have died without remembrance.

Sometimes I fear that I will go on with my life and forget my father entirely. In my mind's eye I picture a family vacation, like those my family used to take when I was young. I am in the car with my parents and brother on a long drive across the country. We come to a rest stop, and my dad gets out of the car. He stands on the curb as the car pulls away. He has come this far but can go no further. The rest of us must continue the journey without him. We drive away, leaving my father behind. And his figure gets smaller and smaller in the distance, until I can't see him anymore.

As we journey on in life without our loved one, we fear that our memories of them will fade away. Because of the corrosive, personality-altering nature of suicidal depression, "by the time suicide occurs, those who kill themselves may resemble only slightly children or spouses once greatly loved and enjoyed for their company."[5] The days, weeks and years following a suicide may be a time of gradually recovering the memories of our loved one, of rediscovering true and lasting remembrances of their life.

So recollections of our loved one take on greater importance. We preserve their memory by assembling scrapbooks and photo albums, by telling and retelling stories, by gathering materials to help us remember who they were and how they lived. In addition, every day we see things that trigger memories of our loved one. It is good for us to write down these memories as we recall them, to preserve them for future generations.

But remembrance goes deeper than this. "The biblical notion of remembrance extends far beyond nostalgic recall," scholars tell us. "Disciplined remembrance is institutionalized in biblical faith because we are called to interpret our present circumstances in light of God's known faithfulness in the past."[6] Forgetfulness is seen in Scripture as a spiritual malady. If we forget our past, we lose direction for the future because we will forget that we are part of a larger story that God is writing throughout human history.

In fact, our remembrance of our loved ones is connected with our remembrance of God. To remember those who have died leads us to remember the One who gave them life in the first place, who gave us the opportunity to know them and love them. Remembrance calls us to meditate on the ways God has been at work in our lives, even in the midst of tragedy and loss.

Furthermore, our remembrance of God is echoed by God's remembrance of us. "The act of remembrance is more than merely a recollection; . . . throughout the biblical text, God's remembrance is the first step in his doing good to those remembered, delivering and encouraging them."[7] For example, in Genesis 8:1 when "God remembered Noah," it is a prologue to Noah's deliverance. So too should we be comforted that God remembers us in our grief and despair. Because he remembers us, we are not forsaken in our distress. He will act on our behalf to comfort us and lead us onward. As we remember God in life, he will remember us in death.

Ultimately, remembrance is not merely backward-looking. Remembrance as a spiritual discipline gives us strength to live in the present and direction to move forward. When our future seems uncertain, remembrance of God's past trustworthiness gives us hope to carry on.

Avoiding the Pitfalls

Somewhere between the extremes of denial and forgetfulness is an appropriate place of memory, where we do not forget our loved one, nor do we cling unhealthily to the desire for their presence. My mother told me of her struggles with this. In Chinese tradition, ancestors who have died remain in some way to help the living continue life. After my father's death, my mom wanted to know what my father was now doing, if he was still around somehow. She occasionally had dreams where he would be back with us. But she came to sense that it wasn't healthy to want Dad to come back, that such hopes could be dangerously close to attempts to communicate with spirits. "I need to let him go," she said.

Many people think of remembrance as a way of keeping their loved ones alive through memories. While there is truth to this, there is something insufficient about it as well. C. S. Lewis railed against this concept:

> What pitiable cant to say, "She will live forever in my memory!" *Live?* That is exactly what she won't do. You might as well think like the old Egyptians that you can keep the dead by embalming them. Will nothing persuade us that they are gone? What's left? A corpse, a memory, and (in some versions) a ghost. All mockeries or horrors. Three more ways of spelling the word *dead*.[8]

Mere remembrance is incomplete and even counterproductive if it degenerates into a mystical sentimentalism. In an attempt to memorialize their loved one, parents of a lost teenager may keep her bedroom exactly as it was. This may not be entirely healthy. Lewis says that this kind of ritual of sorrow, "leaving the empty bedroom exactly as 'the departed' used to keep it," is "like mummification. It made the dead far more dead."[9]

On the other hand, some families go the other extreme and remove all reminders of the lost one. Clothes and belongings are packed up and given away, the bedroom is remodeled into a den, even family portraits and photographs disappear. Neither extreme is healthy. We can find ways to honor the memory of our loved one without either retreating to a static vision of the past or locking our memories away.

One of the hopes of heaven is that we will be reunited with loved ones who have gone before. But we need to be cautious here as well. We should not fall into the trap of imagining that heavenly reunion means that we'll once again have the same kinds of relationships we had here on earth. Lewis says we should not believe "all that stuff about family reunions 'on the further shore,' pictured in entirely earthly terms. . . . That is all unscriptural, all out of bad hymns and lithographs. There's not a word of it in the Bible. And it rings false. We *know* it couldn't be like that. Reality never repeats. The exact same thing is never taken away and given back."[10]

Hope is not restoration to previous modes of life or relationships as we experienced them on earth. The Christian hope is of something very different—*resurrection* into an entirely new and better state of existence. While there is continuity between our identities here and our resurrected bodies, we simply do not yet comprehend what it will be like.

We need to realize that our desire for reunion can be selfish and self-centered. Lewis writes,

> What sort of lover am I to think so much about my affliction and so much less about hers? Even the insane call, "Come back," is all for my own sake. I never even raised the question whether such a return, if it were possible, would be good for her. I want her back as an ingredient

in the restoration of *my* past. Could I have wished her anything worse? Having got once through death, to come back and then, at some later date, have all her dying to do over again?[11]

Another problem with the desire for reunion is that it misplaces the focus of our attention. When considering all things eternal, our focus should be on God, for he alone is eternal and only God can grant us everlasting life. Believers have confidence that we will experience a life beyond this one. There we may well be reunited with others. But that is only a secondary benefit to eternity. The primary reason to look toward eternity is not reunion with loved ones but union with God. That is what we were created for. Lewis concludes, "That's what was really wrong with all those popular pictures of happy reunions 'on the further shore,' not the simple-minded and very earthly images, but the fact that they make an End of what we can get only as a by-product of the true End."[12]

Creating New Memories

Birthdays, anniversaries and holidays can be particularly difficult after a suicide. Holidays are usually supposed to involve happy family cel-ebrations, but what do we do when the holidays are painful for us? What if "celebrating" is the last thing we feel like doing?

The last time I saw my father alive was at Thanksgiving, in the hos-pital after his stroke. He died the next February. The following November I winced when friends and colleagues glibly wished each other, "Happy Thanksgiving!" I felt neither happy nor thankful. That first Thanksgiving without my father, I tangibly felt his absence at our family meal. What could we be thankful for this year?

I found counsel from author Gerald Sittser. A car accident claimed the lives of his wife, his mother and his four-year-old daughter. In one moment three of the most important people in his life were snuffed out. How did he deal with it? He came to realize, "Granted, I did not deserve to lose three members of my family. But then again, I am not sure that I deserved to have them in the first place. . . . Perhaps I did not deserve their deaths; but I did not deserve their presence in my life either."[13]

While I was still sad that my father was gone, I came to be thankful for the time that I had had with him before he died. I was thankful that in his final months he was able to express his love for me. And I continue to be thankful that God provides other friends and family to guide me in my father's absence.

I once asked some other survivors what they now do during the holidays. They told me, "You start new traditions." Counselors agree: "Holidays and birthdays should be observed recognizing the loss but using new family rituals which promote both celebration and healing."[14]

In the years following my father's death, my family has started having Thanksgiving dinner with other families, including one that lost a father shortly before mine. Some survivors light a candle at an empty place setting during a holiday meal. Many regularly visit the grave and use the time as an opportunity to tell stories about the loved one's life. Some families and churches hold a memorial service on the first anniversary of the suicide's death.

It is Chinese custom to have large portraits of departed ancestors in one's house. When my grandfather died, my dad put up a picture of him in the living room. After my dad's death, I put up an 8x10 picture of my father, enlarged from a picture taken at my wedding. It is sometimes unnerving to look at the picture and feel like my dad is watching me, but this too is remembrance. I found other pictures of myself as a child with my father, which I framed and keep at home and at work.

When we practice remembrance, we find ourselves honoring our loved one's life in ways that surprise us. When a new grocery store opened in town, Ellen and I visited it and came away with a number of quirky snacks, including a bag of dried pineapple pieces. One evening as I absent-mindedly munched on a few chunks of pineapple, I realized that this was something my father used to do. He would have an after-dinner snack of dried pineapple or papaya as he watched TV. Eating that food brought him to mind. It was an act of remembrance—not a mere mental memory but a physical reenactment of something of my father's life.

Perhaps this is why the Lord's Supper uses the phrase *"Do this* in remembrance of me," rather than a simple "remember me." To merely remember something is a private, inward mental exercise. But to *do* something in remembrance of another involves an outward commemoration. It becomes an activity of public witness. So remembrance is larger than mental memory. It is the ongoing action of living a transformed life.

Sometimes I wonder if I should think of my dad more often. I fear that I'm dishonoring his memory by not consciously thinking of him from day to day. Since I live two states away, I don't have the immediate daily reminders of my father's absence. For the most part, life goes on. I'm back in the daily routine of home, work, church, friends and activities. People occasionally ask how I'm doing, but as the years have passed, this has tapered off. For the most part we just move on.

I have concluded that going on is also a way of honoring my father. He wouldn't have wanted his death to disrupt my life so I could not do my job or fulfill my responsibilities. Continuing to live is a form of remembrance. While our loved ones are no longer able to be with us, we live on in their stead.

Part II

The Lingering
Questions

Good questions outrank easy answers.
PAUL A. SAMUELSON

Live *the questions now. Perhaps you will then gradually,*
without noticing it, live along some distant day into the answer.
RAINER MARIA RILKE, *LETTERS TO A YOUNG POET*

6

Why Did This Happen?

The hardest part is that we will never be able to ask
the suicide Why?
STEPHANIE ERICSSON, *COMPANION THROUGH*
THE DARKNESS

A core part of the survivor's journey has been described as "an *agonizing questioning,* a tendency to ask repeatedly why the suicide occurred and what its meaning should be for those who are left."[1] More than any other kind of sudden death, suicide raises the "why" questions. Why did she do it? Why did this happen? And why didn't we see it coming?

Our search for answers involves objective questions—what, if anything, caused the suicide? More troubling are the subjective questions: why would he have done this when he had good reasons to live? And on a more cosmic level: Why has this hurt and trauma come about? Is there some purpose behind it?

This chapter will look at the why questions on two levels. The first level is clinical, taking up some of the factors and causes of suicide. The second is more personal, as we grapple with why we look for answers to why suicide happened and whether or not we can ever answer the questions.

Why Do People Kill Themselves?

"For some, suicide is a sudden act. For others, it is a long-considered decision based on cumulative despair or dire circumstance. And for many, it is both: a brash moment of action taken during a span of settled and suicidal hopelessness."[2]

It can be virtually impossible to determine why people kill themselves. Only about one in four leaves a suicide note behind, and even this may not provide any accurate indication of the suicide's state of mind. Many notes offer only vague reasons for the death, if any; some simply indicate that life cannot go on. A twenty-year-old woman who jumped off an office building wrote, "No one is to blame for my doing this. It's just that I could never become reconciled with life itself. God have mercy on my soul."[3]

Those of us left behind often find ourselves searching for a precise event that caused the suicide. We think the act will cease to be incomprehensible if we can identify something as the cause. But we must make a distinction between causes and triggers. A suicide might be triggered by a divorce or the loss of a job, but those may not be the actual causes. After all, many people lose a spouse or a job without considering suicide. Suicidal desires run much deeper, and if one event does not trigger the suicide, another might. So a young woman's suicide should not be blamed wholly on a breakup with her boyfriend. Perhaps the breakup was a trigger, but it was not the only or ultimate cause.

"Suicide is never the result of a single factor or event, but rather results from a complex interaction of many factors and usually involves a history of psychosocial problems," report the Centers for Disease Control and Prevention. "The final precipitating event was not the only cause of a given suicide."[4]

Often the best we can do is understand some of the multiple factors that may have contributed to a loved one's suicide. For example, suicide can be the tragic side effect of domestic violence, not only of battered women but also their children. "Children who witness violence in their home are six times more likely to commit suicide."[5] Those who are divorced are at least two and a half times more likely to attempt suicide.[6] Children of divorce are also at higher risk; 70 percent of teens who attempt suicide have parents who are divorced.[7]

Statistics show that women are two or three times more likely to attempt suicide, but four times as many men actually kill themselves. While women are at least twice as prone to suffer depression, they tend to attempt suicide with less lethal methods such as drug overdoses. Men are more likely to choose more violent methods. Firearms, the most common method of suicide, are involved in 60 percent of all suicides. (In the United States 79 percent of all firearm suicides are white males.)[8]

Two professions that seem to have particularly high rates of suicide are law enforcement and medicine. More police officers die at their own hand than are killed in the line of duty. Nine out of ten cops who kill themselves do so with their own service pistols.[9] Doctors have a suicide rate three times that of the general population. They have easy access to poisonous drugs as well as the medical expertise to use them efficiently.[10] However, suicide can strike within any profession. I heard about a church split that was so acrimonious and painful that the senior pastor took his own life.

In a different category are deaths called "altruistic" suicides, in which a person chooses death to benefit others. Some stories of battlefield sacrifice fall into this category. Some Native Americans have left their tribes in times of famine or hardship, starving or freezing themselves to death in order to conserve limited resources for the benefit of their families.

For most of us, the suicide of our loved one is not among the extreme cases. It is not a political statement such as that of a suicide bomber, nor does it result from involvement in an aberrant religious cult such as Jonestown or Heaven's Gate. These exceptional kinds of suicides lie outside the scope of this book. For most of us, our loved one was simply an ordinary person who chose to end his or her own life.

Whole books have been written on the various causes of suicide, so the material in this section is hardly exhaustive. Here are a few general ways researchers have understood suicide, each of which suggest avenues for suicide prevention.

Medical and biological factors. Studies show that about two-thirds of suicides had suffered from clinical depression or had a history of chronic mental illness.[11] Many have had bipolar (manic-depressive) or borderline personality disorder. Many cases are exacerbated by substance abuse, alcoholism and drug addiction. In an op-ed piece for the *New York Times* author William Styron wrote,

> The pain of severe depression is quite unimaginable to those who have not suffered it, and it kills in many instances because its anguish can no longer be borne. The prevention of many suicides will continue to be hindered until there is a general awareness of the nature of this pain. Through the healing process of time—and through medical intervention or hospitalization in many cases—most people survive depression, which may be its only blessing; but to the tragic legion who are compelled to destroy themselves there should be no more reproof attached than to the victims of terminal cancer.[12]

Psychiatrist Kay Redfield Jamison notes, "Often, people want both to live and to die; ambivalence saturates the suicidal act."[13] These suicides are minds torn in two, part of them wanting desperately to live and another part wanting desperately to die. Those who survive a suicide attempt may later be quite baffled at that "other person" that they were at the time of the attempt.

The organization Suicide Awareness Voices of Education (SAVE) has a campaign using billboards that read: "The #1 Cause of Suicide: Untreated Depression." SAVE, founded by suicide survivors, has worked to help educate the public about suicide warning signs and the medical aspects of depression. "Depression is one of the most common and treatable of mental illnesses, and 80-90% of those suffering from depression can be effectively treated—almost everyone who receives treatment derives some benefit."[14]

Psychological factors. Psychiatrist Karl Menninger suggested that suicides have three interrelated and unconscious dimensions: a wish to kill (the self), due to some degree of self-hatred; a wish to die, arising out of a sense of hopelessness; and a wish to be killed, coming from a sense of guilt.[15] The degree of each factor varies with the individual, but they are often present in some combination.

In many cases, suicidal thoughts arise from a critical lack of self-worth. Young people struggling with eating disorders or homosexual tendencies may consider themselves so repulsive that their intense self-hatred leads to their death. The choice of suicide perhaps expresses a search for peace from internal battles.

Ironically, suicide is a kind of survival mechanism. Most suicides are undertaken as a way to escape the unbearable pain of depression. The depression has so distorted the victim's perception that they are hardly aware that the act of suicide will cause untold grief for their loved ones; the focus is simply on escaping the pain and despair. The agony of depression is so great that the suicide musters the resolve to do away with the pain, at the expense of his or her own life.

An article on one suicide prevention website observes, "When pain exceeds pain-coping resources, suicidal feelings are the result. You can survive suicidal feelings if you do either of two things: (1) find a way to reduce your pain, or (2) find a way to increase your coping resources. Both are possible."[16]

Sociological factors. Nineteenth-century sociologist Émile Durkheim, in his seminal work *Suicide,* argued that suicide is not merely a personal tragedy but sociologically predictable. The more integrated one is in society, whether through marriage or religious or political organizations, the lower the risk of suicide. If an individual is not well integrated into society but is left on his or her own, suicide becomes more likely.

Sociologist Robert Putnam, author of the landmark study *Bowling Alone,* argues that North American society has lost what he calls "social capital," the networks and connections that develop within a civic community. In the last quarter-century, society has tilted toward the individual rather than the communal, and participation in volunteer groups, churches, scout troops, PTAs and even bowling leagues is on the decline. In short, the glue that holds communities and families together is disappearing. We are increasingly a society of isolationists.

Echoing Durkheim's theories, Putnam shows statistically that those who have the least social capital are at greatest risk for suicide. Putnam tracked suicide rates among the elderly and young people across several decades and found that suicide rates among the elderly civic generations declined by half whereas rates among the younger, more socially alienated generations have tripled.[17] Having strong social bonds, whether in marriage, family, church or community, in general seems to prevent malaise, depression and other suicide risk factors. The more socially isolated we become, the higher our risk.

It is widely reported that suicides happen most often on holidays like Christmas. This is actually a myth. "Contrary to previous media reports, suicide rates do not increase during the holiday season. In fact, November and December rank lowest in terms of daily suicide rates."[18] Despite the evidence, this common misconception continues to circulate because we assume that people are particularly lonely and depressed during the holidays. On the contrary, people tend to be less socially isolated during the holidays and have more interaction and support from friends and family members.[19]

Suicide as Philosophical Protest

In *The Myth of Sisyphus* Albert Camus wrote, "There is but one truly serious philosophical problem, and that is suicide. Judging whether life is or is not worth living amounts to answering the fundamental question of philosophy." Camus's observation is a twentieth-century version of the dilemma that humans have faced in every century and civilization. "In the *Dialogue of Pessimism* (a Babylonian work of the fourteenth century B.C.) suicide is the only answer to the problem of life."[20] Whereas most researchers today look at suicide as primarily a medical and psychological issue, throughout the ages people have grappled with it as a philosophical question. Does life have meaning?

If not, some would say, then suicide is a legitimate option.

While most suicides are the result of depression, some may be the result of a nihilistic worldview. Charles Colson and Nancy Pearcey suggest that Ernest Hemingway, one of the greatest novelists of the twentieth century, killed himself as a result of just such a worldview.

> At age sixty-one, after a life of notoriety as a big-game hunter, adventurer, and womanizer, Hemingway deliberately embraced death. He could no longer prove that he was master of his own fate by his daredevil adventures or self-indulgent lifestyle, but he could prove it by controlling the time and means of his own death. On Sunday morning, July 2, 1961, Hemingway loaded his favorite gun, seated himself in the foyer of his Idaho home, braced the butt of the gun on the floor, put the barrel in his mouth, and pulled the trigger.
>
> Neurotic? Sick? Perhaps not. Given his worldview, Hemingway's action was eminently logical. After all, if life is meaningless and despair crouches like a lion at the gate, the best option might be to exit heroically on your own terms. Ernest Hemingway shook his fist at despair one last time by taking control of his own death.[21]

Of course, Colson and Pearcey are speculating; it is likely that biological or genetic factors played a role as well. Hemingway's father, brother and sister all also took their own lives. So did his granddaughter Margaux Hemingway, in 1996. This raises the possibility of a genetic disposition toward depression, melancholia and suicide in the Hemingway family. But biological factors in tandem with a nihilistic worldview certainly may have led to Hemingway's suicide. Given Hemingway's lifelong pursuit of adventure, he may have seen his suicide as the final adventure, the ultimate act of personal autonomy.

As Dietrich Bonhoeffer wrote, "Suicide is a man's attempt to give a final human meaning to a life which has become humanly meaningless."[22]

Suicide Among Artists

William Cowper, one of the greatest Christian poets and hymn writers of the eighteenth century in England, was plagued with a lifelong depression. Despite success and fame, Cowper attempted suicide multiple times, via drug overdose, jumping off a bridge and hanging. Somehow he had the artistic and spiritual ability to pen hymns like "God Moves in a Mysterious Way," yet he died in despair, convinced he had been abandoned by God.

Artistic and creative people, such as painters, writers, musicians and actors, are particularly vulnerable to depression and suicide. The artistic temperament leans toward introspection, and artists tend to be melancholic, depressed and suicidal. Poets and writers are at least four times more likely than the general population to suffer from affective disorders such as manic depression. In many cases depression and suicide are presaged by drug and alcohol abuse. "For actresses like Marilyn Monroe and Judy Garland, it remains unclear whether the cause of death was accidental overdose or suicide."[23]

Often artists resist treatment because they fear that it might reduce their creativity and destroy their talent. Poet Kathleen Norris says that many poets write only when depressed, "which can lead young writers to create situations in their lives that are likely to make them depressed, in order to get the poems."[24] Novelist William Styron, who nearly took his own life, writes,

> Despite depression's eclectic reach, it has been demonstrated with fair convincingness that artistic types (especially poets) are particularly vulnerable to the disorder—which, in its graver, clinical manifestation takes upward of twenty percent of its victims by way of suicide. Just a few of these fallen artists, all modern, make up a sad but scintillant roll call: Hart Crane, Vincent van Gogh, Virginia Woolf, Arshile Gorky, Cesare Pavese, Romain Gary, Vachel Lindsay, Sylvia Plath, Henry de Montherlant, Mark Rothko, John Berryman, Jack London, Ernest Hemingway, William Inge, Diane Arbus, Tadeusz Borowski, Paul Celan, Anne Sexton, Sergei Esenin, Vladimir Mayakovsky—the list goes on.[25]

Researcher Kay Redfield Jamison compiled a list of eighty-two writers and thirty-two artists who took their own lives and another four whose deaths are suspected to be suicides. She also lists twenty-nine writers who attempted suicide, including such luminaries as Joseph Conrad, F. Scott Fitzgerald, Graham Greene, Edgar Allan Poe, Percy Bysshe Shelley and Evelyn Waugh, as well as artists like Paul

Gauguin. Suicide also seems to be prevalent among prominent scientists and mathematicians; Jamison notes that suicide claimed the lives of explorer Meriwether Lewis, computer theorist Alan Turing and chemistry Nobel laureate Emil Fischer.[26]

Suicide Because of Grief

"Another Victim, 3 Months Later," read the headline.[27] When the World Trade Center was attacked by terrorists on September 11, 2001, Joe Flounders died in the collapse of the south tower. His wife, Pat, had struggled with depression even before her husband's death. Friends removed weapons from her home and scheduled counseling appointments for her. But she cancelled the appointments. One December Monday, Pat Flounders shot herself with a small pistol, becoming the first known suicide related to a September 11 victim.

Sometimes it seems that one tragedy leads to others. Six months after the Columbine High School shooting in Littleton, Colorado, a wounded girl's mother walked into a suburban pawn shop. She asked to see a handgun, loaded it with bullets she had brought along and killed herself with a shot to the head.[28] Another six months later, one of Columbine's star basketball players hung himself with an electrical cord in his family's garage.[29] Was his suicide related to the shooting a year earlier? We will never know for certain.

Suicide because of inconsolable grief is a common motif in myth and literature, from Greco-Roman epics to Shakespearean tragedy. Some take their own lives in hopes of reunion with a lost loved one. Sometimes sudden grief in addition to the pressures of life results in suicide. The executive director of a Christian mission organization in Africa, who had struggled with enormous stresses on the mission field, one day learned that his brother and cousin had died in a motorcycle accident. He immediately went home and killed himself by drinking battery acid.[30]

Johann Christoph Arnold tells the story of an army sergeant named Daniel whose sister had been murdered in Los Angeles. The police were unable to solve the crime—so many homicides happened in their precinct that they could spend only four days investigating any death. Daniel was enraged and wanted vengeance, not only on the murderer but on anyone, to achieve some kind of justice for his sister.

Two and a half years later, Daniel was buried next to his sister, having turned his rage inward and taken his own life. His mother said, "He had finally taken revenge—on himself."[31]

Suicide as Atonement?

Western culture usually understands suicide as an act of character weakness or moral failure. But in some cultures suicide is considered a morally acceptable act of atonement for something that has gone wrong. The Japanese ritual suicide of *seppuku* or *hara-kiri* has been historically practiced as an act of removing shame from one's family. While it is less so today, suicide once functioned in Japanese society as a route of honor and even redemptive purification. In some cases an innocent superior would perform seppuku because of the transgressions of a subordinate. A father might even kill himself because of a son's crimes.

This brings other possible answers to the "why?" question. It suggests an alternative interpretation of my father's suicide that is less tragic and more honorable. My family is not Japanese; both of my parents are from Taiwan. But perhaps my father had cultural perspectives similar to the Japanese, and he saw his stroke and physical debilitation as bringing shame upon his family. Perhaps he saw suicide as a way to save the family from dishonor.

But this does not make suicide acceptable. Is it okay for Japanese college students today to kill themselves after failing final exams, to remove shame from their family? No, seppuku is still wrong, or at best a tragic last resort. It should not be accepted as a societal norm.

Some have thought of Jesus' acceptance of crucifixion as a form of seppuku. When Jesus said, "Where I go, you cannot come," some of his skeptics thought he planned to kill himself (John 8:21-22). In a similar vein, some liberal theologians have called Jesus' death a suicide and said that he put himself in harm's way, intentionally knowing his actions would lead to his own death. But this is debatable. Jesus' death does not have the characteristics of most kinds of suicide. Jesus did not go to the cross because he had a death wish. He did not suffer from depression or mental illness, nor did his life exhibit patterns of self-destructive behavior. Rather, he willingly took a death that was meant for others.

In other words, Jesus' death can be called a suicidal act only by the thinnest of definitions. He was more akin to a Secret Service bodyguard who takes a bullet for the president, or a soldier who falls on a grenade to save his company. We do not call these deaths suicides but heroic acts of martyrdom on behalf of others.

Jesus' statement in John 15:13 that the greatest love is laying down one's life for one's friends does not legitimize suicide for Christians today. Because Jesus was God in the flesh, Christ laid down his life on the cross in a way that no one else could ever do. The path of Christian discipleship is living our life in service and love of God and others, not in taking our own life through suicide.

God calls us to choose life, not death. While Peter and Judas both betrayed Jesus, they differed in their response. Judas, in shame and disgrace, chose suicide, which he perhaps saw as the only thing he could do to make things right after handing Jesus over to his death. On the other hand, Peter did not choose suicide, though he may have considered it. Despite his failure and despondency, Peter chose to live. Following the resurrection, Jesus forgave Peter for his denials and restored him to friendship and apostleship. Peter went on to be the primary leader of the early Christian church.

"Judas betrayed Jesus. Peter denied him. Both were lost children," writes Henri Nouwen. "Judas chose death. Peter chose life. I realize that this choice is always before me."[32] If suicide were an acceptable form of atonement, our model for discipleship would be Judas, not Peter. But Christians throughout church history have rejected this. The appropriate response to failure and guilt is not suicide but repentance and restoration. "We are meant to see ourselves in Peter, but no one was ever meant to identify with Judas."[33]

Why We Want to Know Why

> Curiosity is not our only motive: love or grief or despair or hatred is what drives us on. We'll spy relentlessly on the dead: we'll open their letters, we'll read their journals, we'll go through their trash, hoping for a hint, a final word, an explanation, from those who have deserted us—who've left us holding the bag, which is often a good deal emptier than we'd supposed.[34]

Janice told me that after her fiancé's suicide, "I became a detective, like Nancy Drew." In her quest to find out why, she tracked down other survivors and interviewed friends and family members to learn as much as she could, hoping to find out what had caused the suicide. "I was determined to get to the bottom of it," she said. "But there was no bottom to get to."

As one writer puts it, suicide is like "a mystery story without a satisfying solution, since the motives and last thought processes of a 'successful' suicide are for the most part denied us. I might speculate in my own way why he killed himself, but anyone else's guess would be as good as mine."[35]

When something goes wrong, we look for answers. We demand an explanation. We search for reasons that things happened. We ask one another and God the perennial questions, "Why? Why did this happen? Why did he do it? Why didn't I see it coming?"

Six months after my father's suicide, my mom continued to ask me the "why" questions. She had waited so long for him to become a Christian, and she didn't know why, after her years of waiting, he would die when he finally expressed faith. "I don't know if God wanted him to die or if Satan wanted him to die," she said. "I'm so confused."

I didn't know what to say to my mom. It seemed to me that she was attempting to find a context where the suicide made sense, because some divine or demonic force was at work behind it. It reminded me of a column I once read, where Dear Abby was asked if a drunk driving accident was God's fault or Satan's. Abby responded, "Leave both God and Satan out of it. The blame belongs to the drunk driver."

What I must grapple with is not that God wanted my dad to die, or that Satan wanted my dad to die, but that *my dad* wanted to die. I can't know for sure what spiritual forces were at work to influence my father's decision. All I know for certain is that whatever the reasons, my dad decided that death was better than life. That is the reality that survivors are left to deal with.

When we ask "Why?" we may be really asking, "How could they do this to me?" The why question can be answered with a clinical recitation of factors described earlier, like depression and melancholy temperament. The "how could they do this" question is much harder to answer because it suggests rejection and abandonment, that they didn't care about us. What has been helpful to me is the realization that my father did not kill himself to abandon me. He did what he did to end his pain, not to cause pain for me.

Despite all our questioning, perhaps there simply aren't any answers to the why questions. Maybe we *don't* know why and we *can't* know why. Maybe that's all we know. As one survivor wrote,

> I don't know why.
> I'll never know why.
> I don't have to know why.
> I don't like it.
> What I have to do is make a choice about my living.[36]

Somehow we believe that if we can get an explanation for the suicide, we will find peace. In our minds we equate explanations and comfort. But this is a false premise. To have an explanation of the causes of the suicide does not necessarily bring comfort or healing. Answering the intellectual questions may not be what we most need.

Imagine that you have just broken your leg. You are whisked to the hospital emergency room, and in your agony you cry out for an explanation. "Doctor, why did this happen?" you ask.

The doctor looks at you and says, "Well, let me explain it to you.

You tripped and fell and fractured your femur here. The combination of the angle of your fall and the velocity at which you were moving provided sufficient force to crack the bone in two. That's why it happened." The doctor then turns away and leaves the room.

Would that be of much comfort? Of course not. At a time of crisis, an explanation may be helpful, but it is not enough. What is more important is that the bone is set properly so that it can heal correctly. A doctor that provides only a diagnosis without a cure is not fulfilling his duty.[37]

Our search for explanations is really a search for comfort. But suppose a counselor assessed the situation and provided an absolutely certain explanation for the death: "Your daughter's suicide was directly caused by her boyfriend's breaking up with her." Would that provide comfort? Probably not. It would merely serve to increase guilt and blame.

We don't necessarily need answers to the why question. What we need is a doctor to set the broken bone. We need someone to heal our broken heart. Comfort might come from a better understanding of the situation, but it is not limited to it. I do not need to have a full understanding of how a splint should be set in order for a broken bone to heal. If I am being treated for cancer, I don't need complete physiological knowledge of how radiation therapy or chemotherapy works for the treatment to be effective. What I need is the treatment. I need doctors who know how to bring healing and restoration.

In cases of suicide, explanations are not easily obtained and certainty is nearly impossible. Even a suicide note citing specific causes may call the person's state of mind into question. In most cases, we may be able to identify factors that influenced our loved one's decision, but we simply cannot know for sure why the suicide happened. So we must not look to reasons or explanations for comfort, for they provide a false comfort at best.

We must relinquish unrealistic desires for full explanations. Listing reasons to explain a suicide will not bring peace. When Job demanded answers from God, he didn't get the explanations he wanted. He was instead given God's presence. Somehow this was sufficient.

In the aftermath of suicide, we do not have complete understanding of the situation. But we do have a Great Physician who knows how to bring healing and restoration to our broken hearts and broken lives. Healing is not likely to come from torturous analysis of our loved one's last days. We must go to the care of the One who knows how to put us back together.

When You Feel Like It's Your Fault

Janice's fiancé killed himself just three months before their wedding day. He had called her at work one afternoon to tell her how much he loved her. When he didn't show up for dinner, Janice went over to his apartment and saw police and emergency vehicles. He had called 911 to report his own suicide, left his door open so the police could come in, and shot himself.

"I racked my brain looking for answers," Janice remembers. "How could I not know this? I mean, I was studying counseling at the time! Where did this come from? Where was I? I was devastated."

The most difficult aspect for Janice was the guilt. "For years I felt guilty," she says. "I had talked to him every day. Why didn't I know he would do this? I scoured books on suicide and tried to figure out how I missed it." She felt responsible for his death because she was unable to save him.

In our darker moments we answer the "why did this happen" question by pointing the finger at ourselves. We think of ways we might have contributed to the death, signs we didn't see, steps we didn't take to prevent the suicide. This is called survivor's guilt, and it is tremendously common. Virtually all survivors of suicide wrestle with it to some degree.

Some of the most guilt-inducing suicides are carried out by an ex-spouse or former lover who says by means of the suicide, "I can't go on without you." A rebellious teen may lash out at his parents by destroying himself. Worse yet, some suicide notes even name names and say, "This is your fault."

Young children may especially feel that the suicide is their fault, that Mommy or Daddy left because of them. Just as children often blame themselves for their parents' divorce, children tend to think that a family member's suicide is because of something they did.

My father thought that his medical bills were bankrupting the family, and my mother wonders if he killed himself to prevent years of costly institutional care. She agonizes over the possibility that he killed himself for her benefit. I wondered if anticipation of my visit triggered his suicide because he did not want me to see him in his debilitated condition. These are forms of survivor's guilt.

Counselor Becca Cowan Johnson distinguishes between "good guilt" and "bad guilt." If we have done something wrong, the Holy Spirit convicts us of our wrong actions with guilt. "Good guilt is that which we *should* feel—the appropriate response when we have sinned."[38] This is objective guilt, felt in our conscience, and it is appropriate and real. Good guilt comes from God to lead us to repentance and forgiveness.

Bad guilt, on the other hand, comes from unreasonable expectations, either our own or others'. Parents may guilt their children into doing things. Advertisers manipulate us into thinking that we are not good parents if we do not buy the right products for our children. Or we may feel guilty if we eat too much or do not exercise enough. These subjective guilt feelings come from false expectations, not objective guilt from sin. Bad guilt does not come from God.

A man who commits adultery *should* experience guilt for his transgression. This is good guilt. But his innocent wife may feel as if the affair was her fault for not being a better wife. This is bad guilt. The adulterer is the responsible guilty party who needs to repent of his sin. The guilt feelings the wife experiences are false guilt.

In the case of suicide, survivor's guilt is almost always bad guilt. Survivors experience guilt feelings regarding things they might have done to prevent the suicide, but they have not committed any actual offenses worthy of objective guilt. Survivor's guilt is usually unwarranted and unrealistic.

Janice was in graduate school at the time of her fiancé's suicide. Eventually she began to answer calls at a suicide hotline in an effort to save others from doing the same thing. Her supervisor warned her that she would eventually lose a caller to suicide, but Janice resolved that this *would not* happen to her. One day, Janice listened with horror as a young man on the other end of the line shot himself to death. She was devastated once again.

Janice's hotline supervisor wisely and gently told her that the man had chosen to pull the trigger—she had not. It was his choice. She was not responsible for his death. On the contrary, she had done everything possible to save the young man's life.

Eventually Janice came to realize that the guilt she was feeling as a suicide survivor was bad guilt, not good guilt. She had been vindicated, as if found innocent of a crime she did not commit. This was a tremendously freeing truth that enabled her to find healing in her grief. "I realized that I was innocent of his death," Janice said. "It was not my fault."

Those who take their own life are responsible for their final choice. "No person can make another person complete suicide. No person can singlehandedly prevent a suicide unless that person can live without sleep and spend twenty-four hours a day restraining the potential suicide."[39] While we will always wonder whether we could have done anything to prevent the death, we must remind ourselves that it is beyond our power to prevent a suicide.

Often we suspect that we contributed in some way. Perhaps we played some role, major or minor, and contributed some factor that led to their decision. Remember, ultimately it's not your fault! You did not pull the trigger. Responsibility lies finally with the suicide, not with you. They chose to die. Do not blame yourself.

Our guilt feelings, whether good or bad, may be indicators of unfinished business with our loved one. While we did not cause the suicide itself, we may feel remorse over an unresolved argument or a past transgression. Many survivors find it helpful to ask the loved one for forgiveness, perhaps at the casket or gravesite. This can be a step toward forgiving ourselves and releasing ourselves from guilt, real or imagined.

If we have difficulty distinguishing between good guilt and bad guilt, it can be helpful to speak with a pastor, chaplain or counselor about our feelings. While we are not responsible for our loved one's death, our feelings may point us toward other areas of life where we have, in fact, wronged others or God. All of us are imperfect, fallen people, in need of forgiveness and restoration that only God can offer. The promise of God's forgiveness is that "as far as the east is from the west, so far has he removed our transgressions from us" (Psalm 103:12). No matter what we have done, God is able and willing to forgive us of our guilt and restore us.

7

Is Suicide the Unforgivable *Sin*?

We pray for your mercy for those who have killed themselves. We know not their fears, and we thus fear they died alone. They are now yours: in that is our comfort. Comfort all who love them and who will miss their presence.

STANLEY HAUERWAS, PRAYER ON THE OCCASION OF
THE SUICIDE OF A DIVINITY SCHOOL STUDENT

When Diane was six years old, her teenage brother killed himself while away at college. She came home one day to find her father sobbing, having just learned of the death from university representatives. "I knew that cats died and that dogs died, but I didn't think that people died," she remembers. "My family just imploded." Her mother was devastated, and her father sat alone in dark rooms at night crying.

But at first nobody told Diane that her brother had killed himself. Not her family, nor her friends or neighbors. A few months later a neighbor finally explained that the death had been a suicide.

Several years later, when she was about ten, Diane saw a program about life after death. It mentioned that Catholics believe suicides go to hell. Diane was growing up in a Catholic neighborhood, and she now realized why her Catholic friends and neighbors had avoided the subject of her brother's suicide.

"Nobody wanted to tell me because they didn't think I was big enough to handle it," she says. They didn't want her to think about her brother's eternal destiny. After watching the TV program she concluded, *That's what must have happened. He went to hell because he killed himself.* This became a concrete reality to her, and throughout the rest of her growing-up years Diane imagined morbid pictures of her brother in hell.

Images from popular culture reinforce such suspicions. In the movie *What Dreams May Come* a grief-stricken character blames herself for her family's accidental deaths and kills herself in an act of survivor's guilt. A family member in heaven awaits her arrival, only to be told, "She was a suicide. Suicides go to another place." According to the heavenly guide, because suicide violates the natural, God-given order for life, suicides go to hell.

Those of us grieving a suicide are already in pain because our loved one is no longer with us. Then we are further tormented with the possibility that she or he is suffering in hell. We are haunted by terrible questions: What if we will never see our loved ones again? What if they are lost forever? Is suicide the unforgivable sin? Do suicides automatically go to hell?

The Morality of Suicide and the Problem of Forgiveness

Most major world religions have long considered suicide an immoral act. In Islam, suicide warranted eternal damnation. "Muhammad proclaimed that a person who commits suicide will be denied Paradise and will spend his time in Hell repeating the deed by which he has ended his life."[1] In Judaism, a rabbinic text states, "He who destroys himself consciously *(la-daat),* we do not engage ourselves with his funeral in any way. We do not tear the garments and we do not bare the shoulder in mourning and we do not say eulogies for him."[2]

Christianity's stance against suicide can be traced back to the influence of the theologian Augustine. In the fifth century, he declared that suicide was never justifiable, even for those who killed themselves to avoid being raped during the sack of Rome. Suicide, for Augustine, was self-murder and thus a violation of the sixth commandment. "Certainly he who kills himself is a homicide," wrote Augustine.[3]

By the sixth and seventh centuries the church had officially codified its opposition to suicide. Thirteenth-century theologian Thomas Aquinas wrote, "Suicide is always a mortal sin, as being contrary to the moral law and to charity."[4] The church excommunicated suicides and forbade Christian funerals for them. Those who perished at their own hand could not be buried in consecrated ground. In medieval times, suicides' corpses were publicly desecrated by civil authorities as a deterrent to others. In France the bodies of suicides were dragged through the streets. In Germany suicides were put in barrels and floated down rivers so they could not return to their hometown. In Norway suicides were buried in the forest with criminals. Until recently Amish communities buried suicides outside the boundaries of the community cemetery.[5]

Shakespeare's *Hamlet* is something of a case study in traditional attitudes toward death and forgiveness for sin. While Hamlet is most known for his "To be or not to be" soliloquy in act 3, Hamlet's first soliloquy in act 1, scene 2, is actually the play's most explicit reference to suicide. There Hamlet laments, "O . . . that the Everlasting had not fix'd His canon 'gainst self-slaughter!"[6] Hamlet is distressed that God has written a law against suicide, because he is in despair and considering it.

Then in act 1, scene 5, Hamlet encounters the ghost of his father, who has been murdered by Hamlet's uncle Claudius. While the king slept, his brother poured poison into his ear. "Thus was I, sleeping, by a brother's hand of life, of crown, of queen at once dispatched," says the ghost of King Hamlet. The ghost emphasizes that his murder was made more tragic by the fact that he was asleep at the time of death, preventing him the opportunity to repent of his sins.

Cut off even in the blossoms of my sin,
Unhouseled, disappointed, unaneled,

No reckoning made, but sent to my account
With all my imperfections on my head.

Because Hamlet's father died without confession, his spirit was
denied entry to heaven and is instead "doomed for a certain term to
walk the night, and for the day confined to fast in fires."[7]

Later on, in act 3, scene 3, Hamlet comes upon his father's murderer, Claudius, kneeling in prayer considering his evil deeds. Hamlet
realizes that this would be an opportune time to avenge his father:
"Now might I do it pat, now 'a is a-praying." He draws his sword,
ready to kill Claudius, but then reconsiders.

And so 'a goes to heaven.
And so am I revenged. That would be scanned:
A villain kills my father, and for that,
I, his sole son, do this same villain send
To heaven.[8]

His uncle is presumably repenting of his sins and being forgiven of
his crimes. Hamlet reasons that if he were to strike him dead now,
Claudius would go directly to heaven in his forgiven state. So he
withdraws, plotting to kill his uncle at a later time.

If we put all these pieces together, we see that Hamlet (and presumably most citizens of medieval Christendom) believed that to die unfor-
given, without confession of sin, leads to damnation or at least
purgatory, while those who die having repented of their misdeeds are
qualified for heaven. This view of repentance and forgiveness implies
that Claudius is bound for heaven only until his next evil deed. He is
then doomed until he is able to repent once again for all his wrongs.

Based on such an understanding, many Christians throughout
church history have considered suicide an unforgivable sin because it
allows no possibility of repentance. But virtually all deaths occur
without wholly cleansed consciences. If someone dies from a sudden
heart attack, chances are that person died without asking for forgiveness for any number of sins.

Dietrich Bonhoeffer argued that to expect complete repentance in
the final moment of life is unrealistic, observing, "Many Christians

have died sudden deaths without having repented of all their sins."[9] Another commentator says, "Suicides are not alone in dying in an unrepentant state: others—perhaps most of us—will die with unrepented sins."[10] Ethicist and theologian Gilbert Meilaender writes,

> Contrary to what Christians have often believed, such rational suicide does not necessarily damn one. The suicide dies, so to speak, in the moment of sinning, without opportunity to repent. But then, so may I be killed instantly in a car accident while plotting revenge against an enemy of mine. God judges persons, not individual deeds, and the moment in one's life when a sinful deed occurs does not determine one's fate.[11]

Christians affirm that at conversion God forgives all our sins—past, present and future, once and for all. This suggests we need not be as troubled over whether our loved one has asked for forgiveness for all their sins before the suicide. Christian salvation is not dependent on whether a person was able to "wipe the slate clean" at the moment of death, but rather whether the person was walking in relationship with God in life.

Suicide in the Bible

The Bible records seven acts of suicide. Abimelech, mortally wounded, asked his armor bearer to run him through with his sword (Judges 9:52-54). Samson pushed aside the supporting pillars of a temple, killing himself and all within it (Judges 16:28-31). King Saul, wounded in battle, fell on his own sword, and his armor bearer did likewise (1 Samuel 31:4-6). Ahithophel hanged himself when his counsel was rejected (2 Samuel 17:23). King Zimri set his palace on fire and burned himself to death (1 Kings 16:18). The only case of suicide in the New Testament is Judas Iscariot, who hanged himself after betraying Jesus (Matthew 27:3-5; Acts 1:18).

All these accounts are straightforward narratives; none offers any particular comment on the act of suicide. In fact, while the Bible condemns murder in general, it nowhere condemns suicide in particular. The strange silence of Scripture on the morality of suicide has led some people to either one of two extremes. Some read far too much into these passages, seeing suicide as the unforgivable sin though it is not so described. Others minimize the acts entirely, arguing that because these suicides are not condemned, suicide is morally neutral or excusable.

The truth lies in between. Even though Scripture does not explicitly condemn suicide, the narratives all depict the suicide's fate negatively. Scripture's silence does not mean tacit approval or indifference.[12] The stories were meant to be instructive to future generations, portraying biblical suicides not as examples to be followed but rather as cautionary warnings of how not to go.

While Scripture casts all acts of suicide in a negative light, this does not mean that suicide always eternally separates the victim from God. On the contrary, Christian physician and medical examiner John Roos notes, "I have pointed out to the bereaved that Samson's suicidal death (Judges 16) did not exclude him from [the] list of the 'faithful' in Hebrews 11, and have found solace in this example."[13]

We should also note that according to Matthew 12:31-32, the "unforgivable sin" is blasphemy against the Holy Spirit. Most interpreters understand this as attributing the works of God to the power of the devil. There is no connection anywhere in Scripture between suicide and a sin that cannot be forgiven.

Interestingly enough, the Bible also records stories of at least seven people who despaired of life but did not go the way of suicide. These include Rebekah (Genesis 27:46), Rachel (Genesis 30:1), Moses (Numbers 11:10-15), Elijah (1 Kings 19:4), Job (Job 6:8-13; 10:1-22), Jonah (Jonah 4:3, 8) and the apostle Paul (2 Corinthians 1:8-9). These are positive role models for us, in contrast to those who chose death instead of life. "Given the clear examples throughout the Bible of men and women who thought about killing themselves and chose not to, we should follow their example."[14]

Hope for the Suicide

Christians, especially pastors and chaplains, often find themselves caught in a tension, wanting to offer comfort to a grieving family but unable to affirm with any confidence that the lost one is in heaven. What I have found helpful is to understand that salvation and forgiveness of sins are more a *relational* matter of being a follower of God than a *transactional* matter of mechanically repenting for every misdeed.

Many Christian traditions agree that a person will not be judged on the nature of his or her death but rather on the nature of his or her life. One act does not necessarily invalidate a person's entire life, especially if an act of desperation is completely uncharacteristic of that person's demonstrated moral identity. "There is an important distinction to be maintained between basic moral dispositions and single actions," writes New Testament scholar Luke Timothy Johnson. "Specific acts must be placed within the context of a person's character as revealed in consistent patterns of response."[15] A person's fundamental disposition is more defining of his or her moral character than an isolated act.

In other words, the single act of suicide does not negate a person's entire moral identity. If a loved one has aimed to live a life of Christian discipleship, of faith, hope and love, then we can see the act of suicide as an aberration. In such cases we may well understand the suicide as a tragic twist of an otherwise good life, not the inevitable end of a self-destructive life.

Suicide also raises the question of intent. If suicidal people are overwhelmed by the agony of their despair, are they morally responsible for their choice? Does God provide grace for those who do not fully know what they are doing? This suggests a larger question: whether God accepts those who do not have the capacity to make a conscious decision to believe in God, such as infants, mentally handicapped people or those with Down syndrome.

Jesus said that those who would enter the kingdom of God must become like little children. Many Christians interpret this as meaning that God's grace extends to the mentally handicapped, who often display the kind of childlike faith and trust that Jesus described, even if they are incapable of articulating explicit faith in God. Some theologians have argued that God—being perfectly fair and just, as well as loving and merciful—is able to discern how people *would have* responded to his invitation to follow him had they had the mental capacity to understand and choose.

Simply put, some people truly desire to be with God. They want to participate in a continual, personal, active relationship with him. Heaven, then, is the natural result of that relationship. They want to go to heaven because they want to be with God.

On the other hand, other people just do not care about God. They do not think about spiritual things and have no interest in having a relationship with God. Why, then, would they *want* to go to heaven? If heaven is the ultimate culmination of all things spiritual and godly, then those who do not have any desire to be in relationship with God would have no reason to want to be in heaven. Christians throughout the centuries have maintained that God does not *send* people to hell; rather, people say no to God and choose the path away from him on their own volition and free will. Those who do not care about the things of God in this life continue on that trajectory in the life to come.

This may be of little consolation to those who grieve the death of a loved one and who are uncertain of that person's eternal condition. But it can provide hope to those of us who grieve a suicide. Imagine that all his life Bill has been a faithful believer in God. He has been a committed Christian, seeking to live a life in relationship with God and wanting to follow his will. Of course he does so imperfectly and experiences ups and downs in his daily life, but his aim is to walk with Jesus as best he can.

But for some reason, despair overtakes Bill. Perhaps there has been a chemical disturbance somewhere in his brain. Perhaps he has lost his job, or his wife or children, and he sinks into a severe clinical depression. He is beyond consolation, and his friends wonder if he's even really the same person he was before. One night, in utter despondency, to end his pain, Bill takes his own life.

How should his loved ones think of his passing? What will the pastor say at his funeral?

Christians do not hold the false hope that all who die regardless of faith will go to heaven. We take Jesus seriously when he says that there are two paths, one to life and another to destruction, and people will wind up in one of two eternal destinies (Matthew 25:31-46). We take seriously the reality that there is a heaven and a hell, and all of us will someday see one or the other.[16]

But that destiny is never arbitrarily determined. In Charles Dickens's *A Christmas Carol* Jacob Marley's ghost tells Ebenezer Scrooge, "These are the chains I forged in life." Our decisions in this life forge our future destiny.

We also affirm that God will be fair. He is a righteous judge. In human courts, the best judges take all evidence into account. God, infinite in knowledge, knows all of Bill's circumstances. He knows his heart and commitment to faith. He will respond to Bill's life and death with complete fairness and understanding.

If a person dies of cancer, God does not hold that cancer against him. God considers the state of his soul, not merely his ravaged body. If the person enters into eternal life, his body is supernaturally resurrected to a new body, free from cancer and any other earthly frailties. Likewise, God will consider the state of a suicide's soul, not merely the mind which may have been misled and confused at the time of the suicide. God is just and perfect in wisdom, and he is able to tell which acts and beliefs were truly volitional and which were not. Should that person be welcomed into eternal life, her mind will be restored, healed of all depression and given full capacity to renew a joyous relationship with God.

The Bible even offers hope for the person who has had a lifelong trajectory away from God. The Bible records that two thieves were crucified along with Jesus, one on either side. One hurled insults at Jesus, but the other called to Jesus for mercy: "Jesus, remember me when you come into your kingdom." Jesus replied, "I tell you the truth, today you will be with me in paradise" (Luke 23:42-43).

This thief most likely was a career criminal, a bandit who had lived as a predator on society; he probably was never part of Jewish religious culture. He had given no thought to God, only to what he could get away with. But he had a change of mind and heart in his last moments. Jesus tells him (and us) that repentance, even on one's deathbed, is sufficient. God is merciful. Those who call upon the Lord will be saved.

This gives us hope for even the person who has spent his entire life without a concern for God. Imagine that Bill is an entirely godless atheist who never once considers God. Not only does he ignore God, he actively mocks him and those who believe in him. He takes pleasure in the things of this world with no thought or regard for the welfare of others.

One day it all catches up with him. He crosses the line one time too many, and the game is up. Hunted by the police, with squad cars closing in, Bill finally has a change of heart. He takes a few final minutes for silent surrender to the God of the universe whom he only now acknowledges. He tells God that there's no way he can atone for all the wrongs he has done, and the only way he can make things right is to remove himself from this world. So he places a gun to his head and pulls the trigger.

Is there hope for Bill in this scenario? If we believe the Bible, including Jesus' words to the thief on the cross next to him, we must say yes, there is hope even for a penitent criminal suicide. The majority of suicides leave no note behind, no record or indication of their final mental state. Who is to say whether or not those suicides, in their final moments, did business with God and made things right? The miracle of salvation is that God can forgive even the most heinous sinner. No one is beyond hope.

The Comfort of Not Knowing

Diane, whose brother killed himself in college, had assumed the traditional perspective that all suicides go to hell. But eventually she realized that this may not be the case. She spent a summer taking care of a missionary family's kids. One day Diane said in passing, "Well, I know my brother is in hell because he committed suicide."

The missionary mother didn't say anything at first, but the next day she gently challenged Diane: "That might be something you want to look into a little bit more, because I'm not really sure that it's true."

"I just never really thought about it," Diane remembers. "She opened the door for me to look at that again." Diane's mind was opened to the possibility that suicide is not an unforgivable sin. Perhaps suicides don't automatically go to hell. "I started to see that suicide might be a sin, but it's a sin like other sins. It doesn't necessarily mean that this person is in hell. I don't know where my brother was at. I just don't know. But honestly, I'm grateful to be in a place of not knowing."

There is an odd sort of comfort in ignorance. This doesn't mean that our loved ones are actually in hell and we just delude ourselves into thinking they aren't. Nor is it a blind insistence that they are in heaven. No, it is a simple resignation to the reality that some things are beyond human knowledge, at least in this life. We simply do not know the ultimate fate of those who are gone. But God gives us hope. Not certainty, but hope.

Theologian Lewis Smedes was asked, "Is suicide unforgivable? What is the biblical hope and comfort we can offer a suicide victim's family and friends?" His response was: "Will Jesus welcome home a believer who died at her own hands? I believe he will, tenderly and lovingly. My biblical basis? It is the hope-giving promise of Romans 8:32, that neither life nor death can separate the believer from the love of God in Christ Jesus." Jesus died for all of our sins, including suicide.

Smedes points out that most people who choose suicide do not mean to sin against God. Those who attempt suicide "do not so much choose death as stumble down into it from a steep slope of despair." Many who kill themselves are "not people sticking their fists in the face of God. These are children who look in their own faces and hate what they see." The true killers, says Smedes, are despair, depression, hopelessness and self-loathing. These are our most urgent problems, not the question of the morality of suicide. We should worry less about whether suicides go to heaven and more about how to help the suicidal find hope and meaning.[17]

Even Catholicism, often thought to consign all suicides to hell, holds out hope for the suicide. The *Catechism of the Catholic Church* says, "We should not despair of the eternal salvation of persons who have taken their own lives. By ways known to him alone, God can provide the opportunity for salutary repentance."[18]

We can find comfort that in God's justice our loved one's actions may be seen in light of their circumstances. "Grave psychological disturbances, anguish, or grave fear of hardship, suffering, or torture can diminish the responsibility of the one committing suicide."[19]

It is not for us to speculate on a suicide's final destination. I have stopped worrying about my father's eternal fate. It does me no good to wonder about things that are impossible to know. "Ultimate judgments about the person are not therefore ours to make, and we can condemn the act of suicide without claiming to render such a verdict."[20] While I am hopeful that I will see my father again someday, I cannot cling to a false hope and claim with certainty that he is in heaven. That is not for me to say.

It is comforting, however, to know that the God of the universe is good and just and can be trusted to do the right thing. He is both righteous and merciful, and he understands the pain of both the victims and the survivors of suicide. Only God knows the fate of those we grieve. Ultimately we must place our trust in his goodness and mercy.

Suicide as Tragedy

In considering the wrongfulness of suicide, we can be tempted to make one of two equal and opposite errors. One is to think of suicide as an unforgivable sin. The other is to not consider it a sin at all. The first position makes the error of treating suicide too harshly; the second makes the error of treating it too lightly.

A more balanced position is to consider suicide a tragedy. In literary terms, a tragedy is the story of a tragic protagonist who is undone by a fatal flaw. "Often the tragic hero comes to a moment of perception, usually an insight into what he or she has done wrong to set the forces of retribution in motion. As the tragic plot unfolds, the tragic hero becomes gradually isolated from others. Tragedies typically end with the death of the hero."[21] A tragedy is a situation where a good person's human frailties and failures lead to self-destruction.

The suicides recorded in the Bible, especially the stories of King Saul and Judas, fit this archetype of tragedy. Saul's life, like a Greek or Shakespearean tragedy, can be charted as rise and fall, from the heroic young king to the troubled and ultimately doomed warrior. Judas, likewise, is a once-trusted confidant who is seduced into treachery and self-destruction. Judged by moral categories, their actions are simply wrong and sinful, but reading with a literary sensibility, we see in their lives the motif of tragedy.

While all suicides are tragic to some degree, different circumstances and reasons for suicide make us interpret individual suicides differently. A young mother whose baby died in an accident might kill herself out of grief and a desire to be reunited with her child. Though we lament her decision, we are far more sympathetic with her than with Hitler's suicide in his bunker at the end of World War II. Hitler's death was the result of a life wasted in evil, while the young mother's death is a catastrophic expression of maternal love.

"In tragedy, sin is surely one of the forces at work, but it is by no means the only force and sometimes not even the most obvious one."[22] In other words, suicide is wrong and is a serious sin, but not one that is unforgivable. The motif of tragedy compels us to understand our loved one's final act in the context of the full story of his or her life. In the tragedy of suicide, our loved ones fought against an enemy within. They lost their battle against themselves. While part of them may well deserve God's judgment, another part may well receive God's mercy.

Psychologist John White writes, "Let us grant that suicide is not only tragic but sinful. Let us accept that life is a precious gift from God and that issues of life and death belong to their Author. But let us look on those who take their lives with the same compassion with which Jesus looked on all sinners. Indeed if compassion is called for, surely some suicide victims call for more compassion than other sinners."[23]

Are Suicides Martyrs?

Some recent writers have claimed that early Christians so honored martyrdom that they celebrated and even pursued their own deaths. Arthur Droge and James Tabor have equated suicide with martyrdom in their book *A Noble Death,* calling them both forms of "voluntary death." These and other revisionists say that because the early martyrs' deaths were considered praiseworthy, so too should we today affirm and celebrate such "voluntary deaths" as physician-assisted suicide and euthanasia.

However, this argument is a gross misapplication of a mistaken reading of history. Death by martyrdom during persecution by Christianity's opponents is hardly comparable to most contemporary suicides. Most martyrs did not take their own lives; they were killed by their oppressors. Even if they gave up their own lives willingly, this doesn't mean that they had a death wish. If they had not been persecuted by the Romans, they would not have been killed.

Meilaender clarifies:

> Christians generally forbade suicide, but they honored their martyrs. Why? How can they honor someone whose own choice so certainly results in her death? They honor the martyr because she does not *aim* at her death. She aims to be faithful to God, foreseeing as a likely result the loss of her life. Forbidding suicide and honoring martyrs, Christians recognized life as a real but not ultimate good—a great good, but not the highest good.[24]

Most of our loved ones did not take their own life because they were being threatened on account of their faith. Someone else did not kill them. In most cases, the suicides we grieve were killed by their own volition, without coercion or persecution from without. So we cannot equate our loved ones' actions with those of the ancient martyrs. That is simply a category mistake. True martyrs are still dying for their faith around the world today, and to equate their actions with suicide dishonors them.

In rare cases, true martyrs may kill themselves in order to affirm a higher commitment to God. During World War II, an orthodox Jewish girls' school in Nazi-occupied territory had been spared extermination in order to provide sexual services to the Gestapo. To avoid being violated, the students, ranging from age twelve to eighteen, gathered together with their teachers, recited a final prayer and poisoned themselves to death. They are now known as "the ninety-three maidens."[25]

While some theologians like Augustine would still condemn such deaths, philosopher Robert N. Wennberg argues that this sort of suicide "declares that one lives by a higher loyalty and thereby sanctifies the name of God. In ending one's life in these circumstances, one affirms in death the values and the commitments to God by which one lived. In such circumstances suicide is not a repudiation of those values but an affirmation of them."[26]

What About the Criminal Suicide?

My friend Lauren called one day and asked if I had heard about a murder-suicide that had taken place the previous weekend. Kathleen Roskot, a nineteen-year-old sophomore at Columbia University, had been found murdered in her dorm room. Shortly afterward her boyfriend, Thomas Nelford, threw himself in front of a subway train and killed himself. Lauren, a graduate student at Columbia, was writing an article about the situation, and her editor, a secular Jew, had taken the position that it was good that the murderer killed himself. Good riddance, in essence.

Lauren wanted to know what I thought of the murderer's suicide, from the standpoint of the Christian faith. It seemed to me that we couldn't say that the suicide in any sense resolved the tragedy of the murder; if anything, it compounded the pain—one tragedy on top of another.

What do we make of the suicide of a murderer? Regarding the perpetrator's eternal destiny, we must plead ignorance, since only God knows the state of his soul. But it seems to me that our stance toward him should be lament, not satisfaction or vindictiveness. In this case, we grieve for the female student as the victim of a senseless murder. And in a different way, we also grieve for the male student as the victim of a senseless self-murder.

I was reminded of the April 1999 killings at Columbine High School, when Eric Harris and Dylan Klebold killed twelve classmates and a teacher and then killed themselves. The pastor who officiated at Dylan Klebold's funeral read 2 Samuel 18:33, where David laments the death of his treasonous son Absalom in one of the most emotional cries in all of Scripture: "O, my son Absalom! My son, my son!" Even when the death is that of a murderer, we grieve.

I told Lauren, "Even a murderer's life is still a life. There is intrinsic value of all life regardless of moral behavior. Because human beings were created in the image of God, the loss of any life is to be lamented."

No matter how fallen or corrupted, every human being was once an innocent child. Christians affirm that all people bear the image of God. Therefore any loss of human life is a tragedy to be mourned. As John Donne said, "Any man's death diminishes me, because I am involved in mankind."[27] Because Christians affirm the inherent dignity of every human being, because we believe in the sanctity of all life, we cannot take glee in the deaths of criminals and murderers. We rather grieve that things went so horribly wrong in the perpetrators' lives that they came to harm others. We must not demonize them and see them only in terms of evil. Rather, they too were the victims of evil. Even somebody like Hitler, who seems to us the very embodiment of evil, was a human being created in the image of God; his awful, tragic life is also to be mourned.

Here is how Lauren concluded her article:

In wrestling with how to respond to the suicide of a murderer, we might do well to recall a violent death recounted in Hebrew Scripture. We learn in the book of Exodus that after the Red Sea parted, the Israelites crossed to the other side, but when the Egyptians tried to chase them, the walls of the sea collapsed and the Egyptians drowned. According to a midrash, the angels in heaven began to cheer, but God silenced them, saying: "You may not cheer. The Israelites are free and my plan for their redemption is unfolding, but some of my other children are dead, so you may not cheer."

God doesn't ask the angels to cry for the Egyptians. But he does remind them that the death of even the vilest of his creations is a somber moment.[28]

We often forget that this earth is caught in a cosmic conflict between good and evil, with powers and principalities at work beyond our detection. One theologian writes, "In the Christian view, then, the earth has been literally sieged by a power outside itself. There is a power of pure evil which now affects everything and everybody on the earth. . . . We are, like Normandy in World War II, caught in the crossfire of a cosmic battle. And on battlefields, as you know, all sorts of terrible things happen."[29] Humanity is caught in the crossfire, and in any war there are casualties. Human victims of murder and suicide are casualties in the battle waged between God and Satan.

We will never know Thomas Nelford's final thoughts as he stood on the subway platform. The killing of Kathleen Roskot may have happened in a fit of rage, and afterward he very well may have come to understand the horrible magnitude of his crime. Perhaps his suicide was merely a cowardly way to escape criminal prosecution. Or perhaps he decided that the only way to atone for his girlfriend's death was to pay with his own life. We simply cannot know. But either way, he was still a person created in the image of God, and we lament his taking of his life. Perhaps his parents would identify with Dylan Klebold's parents in David's lament: "If only I had died instead of you, my son, my son!"

Forgiving the Suicide

There is another sense in which survivors wonder if suicide is unforgivable. In taking their own lives, our loved one has hurt us immeasurably. Can we bring ourselves to forgive them?

Without excusing their act, we can say what Jesus said on the cross: "Father, forgive them, for they know not what they do." Those who choose suicide usually don't realize how much trauma and grief they inflict on us survivors. Even though we feel hurt, angry and betrayed, we can come to forgive them because their final thoughts were preoccupied with ending their own pain. They did not know what they were doing to us.

This may not be something we can do quickly or easily. It may take months or years. We may or may not sense the need for it. Chris, who had learned to forgive a man who shot him and left him for dead, said: "There is a very pragmatic reason for forgiving. When we are wronged, we can either respond by seeking revenge, or we can forgive. If we choose revenge, our lives will be consumed by anger. When vengeance is served, it leaves us empty. Anger is a hard urge to satisfy and can become habitual. But forgiveness allows us to move on."[30]

We survivors of suicide know we have been wronged. We have been victimized by our own loved one, in an act of intense betrayal. But there is no point in harboring resentment. We cannot seek revenge. Our loved ones have already sought vengeance upon themselves. So we grieve them as victims, and we forgive them for the wrong they perpetrated on themselves and on us. After all, if suicide is forgivable by God, it can be forgivable by us. We can forgive them, for they knew not what they did.

8

Where Is God When It Hurts?

I fired God that day. I hated God that day. I still hate God.
But now I'm forced to believe in some kind of god,
simply because if I am to continue living, the silence
of the Great Alone is too much.

STEPHANIE ERICSSON, *COMPANION THROUGH*
THE DARKNESS

How can we believe in God after a suicide? For some survivors, suicide is the final evidence of the absence of God. As proof positive, skeptics point to cases where Christians lose hope and kill themselves. Such a suicide only confirms the suspicion that Christianity can't be true. God can't exist. After all, look at what happened to them.

When tragedy strikes, our core beliefs are shaken. The world appears meaningless; our lives seem hopeless. If we believe in God, we begin to wonder if God is still there, or if he ever existed. We doubt that God cares or that he is good. We think that because God didn't prevent the suicide from happening, God must not have cared about our loved one's plight. We equate God's inactivity with his uncaring. We conclude that if God cared, he would have done something. Our real question, then, is not how God could let this happen, but why doesn't God care about us?

Our fear is that God is cruel, that he has set in motion a cold, heartless universe where our loved ones are left to their own devices, abandoned, hopeless and vulnerable to suicidal despair. C. S. Lewis, grieving the death of his wife, wrote, "Not that I am (I think) in much danger of ceasing to believe in God. . . . The conclusion I dread is not, 'So there's no God after all,' but "So this is what God's really like. Deceive yourself no longer.'"[1] Friends attempted to console him by saying that his wife is "in God's hands." Lewis retorted, "But she was in God's hands all the time, and I have seen what they did to her here."[2]

Is it possible to believe in God when this world is so filled with pain and suffering? Is God doing this to us? Is he tormenting us? Where is God when it hurts?

A Tale of Two Soldiers

During World War II, a young Viennese Jew named Hans Maier fled from Austria to Belgium, where he joined the resistance movement. In 1943 Maier was caught by the Nazis, taken prisoner and tortured by the SS. They bound his hands behind his back and pulled them up until his arms dislocated, and then they flogged him at length. He spent the next two years in Auschwitz and other concentration camps. He survived the Holocaust but was haunted ever after by it.

Twenty-two years later, Maier wrote about his Holocaust experiences under the pseudonym Jean Améry. In spite of great fame and success, he attempted suicide in 1974. Améry began work on a "Meditation on Suicide" in 1975 and the next year delivered a series of radio addresses on the topic, which were eventually published as a book, *On Suicide*. There he wrote, "The suicide becomes a figure just as exemplary as the hero. Someone fleeing the world is not worse than someone who conquers the world—perhaps even a trace better."[3] In 1978 Améry killed himself.

Jürgen Moltmann was born in Hamburg, Germany, in 1926. Like most young German men his age, Moltmann fought for the Nazis in World War II. He was captured by the British in 1945 and was held in prisoner-of-war camps in Belgium and Scotland until 1948. His hometown had been destroyed, and his faith in the German Reich had been shattered. "I felt abandoned by God and human beings, and the hopes of my youth died," Moltmann writes. "I couldn't see any future ahead of me."

Then an American chaplain gave him a Bible, and Moltmann began to read it. He came across the Old Testament psalms of lament and Luther's translation of Psalm 39: "I have fallen dumb and have to eat up my suffering within myself." Then he came to the story of the crucifixion of Jesus,

> and when I came to Jesus' death cry I knew: this is the one who understands you and is beside you when everyone else abandons you. "My God, why have you forsaken me?" That was my cry for God too. I began to understand the suffering, assailed and God-forsaken Jesus, because I felt that he understood me. And I grasped that this Jesus is the divine Brother in our distress. . . . I became possessed by a hope when in human terms there was little enough to hope for. I summoned up the courage to live, at a point when one would perhaps willingly have put an end to it all.[4]

Moltmann lived on to become one of Germany's foremost Christian theologians of the twentieth century.

Two men, born five years apart, went through the same horrific war. But they responded in very different ways. Even though he had survived the war, when faced with the pain and agony of the world Jean Améry turned to suicide. Faced with similar pain and disillusionment, Jürgen Moltmann instead embraced belief in God. A former resistance fighter chose death, while a former Nazi soldier chose life.

Why the difference? Why could Améry find no hope for living, despite his survival of the Holocaust? Perhaps Améry never understood what Moltmann had grasped. The sufferings of the world do not confirm God's absence; rather, God makes his presence known through suffering.

The Suffering of God
Most world religions and philosophies believe that God, if he exists, cannot feel pain. But Christians believe that through the person of Jesus Christ, God has entered the human experience of suffering.

God has become the suffering God.

Christian philosophers and theologians have long wrestled with whether God can truly suffer. According to classical theology God is "impassible," meaning that the divine nature is not subject to change or loss. If God suffers, he does not do so in a way that diminishes his Godhood. God does not suffer out of weakness or vulnerability, as if his divine omnipotence were at all threatened. Rather he suffers out of his love for and identification with his creatures. Because people in a fallen world suffer, God too suffers.

But God does not merely suffer in a metaphorical or analogical sense. Christian theology holds that Jesus was both fully divine and fully human. Because Jesus is both the Son of God and the Son of Man, he is both God and man, and thus God suffers as a true human being.

Through the incarnation of Jesus Christ, "God actually experiences something new and knows first hand—as one of us mortals—suffering and anguish within a fallen world," writes theologian John Cavadini. "The Incarnation, Passion, and Resurrection are God's answer to the problem of evil, and so a properly precise portrayal of the Incarnation—not the attribution of suffering to the divine nature—is the appropriate Christian defense against the charge that God is an eternal bystander. In Christ, God truly enters into radical historical solidarity with human suffering."[5]

In other words, God's suffering is not theoretical. His knowledge of suffering is experiential. He does not just know *about* our suffering. Rather, he knows through Jesus' experience what human suffering is.

Some Christians have thought that because God is unchanging he cannot feel pain or be hurt. In such a portrait God comes across as cold, aloof and uncaring. But this is not the biblical picture of God. This concept of God comes more from the Greek philosophy of Stoicism than from Scripture.

The biblical view is that God experiences emotions of both joy and sorrow. The Hebrew portrait of God is far more relational than that of the Greeks; the God of the Bible weeps, mourns, grieves and hurts. This is no mere anthropomorphism; we are not merely projecting human emotions on an emotionless God. Quite the reverse. Given that we human beings are created in the image of God, our emotions point to the fact that God is passionately emotive. While the Greeks saw emotions as human foibles unworthy of a deity, the Hebrews saw our emotions as consistent with God's identity. Our emotions derive from his. Our human emotions are actually evidence that God has emotions.

In fact God feels emotions like joy and grief in a greater, more complete and perfect way than we ever could. We shield ourselves from the full force of grief with defense mechanisms that protect us from being overwhelmed. But God is open to the total magnitude of loss. If we suffer, God suffers more. If we are in pain, he experiences pain more fully and completely than we ever could.

A fellow survivor of suicide told me that she had realized that God was grieving with her in her loss, that God cared for her brother just as much as she did.

"More," I said, with a lump in my throat. "God cares even more than we do." God grieves for our loved ones even more than we ever could because he is infinitely more capable of grief. Our grief is limited. God's grief is absolute.

Scripture portrays God as a God of compassion. Psalm 116:5 says, "Our God is full of compassion," and Psalm 145:9 says that he "has compassion on all he has made." *Compassion* literally means "to suffer with." When we suffer, God suffers with us. He is not distant and aloof. He is present with us, sharing our suffering.[6]

Moltmann says Jesus' suffering on the cross means that "God could be beside us in our suffering and with us in our pain." It shows evidence of God's solidarity with us, that Christ is our divine brother who takes on our sufferings. "God always helps first of all by suffering with us," says Moltmann. "No suffering can cut us off from this companionship of the God who suffers with us. The God of Jesus Christ is the God who is on the side of the victims and the sufferers, in solidarity with them."[7]

Jesus is described as "a man of sorrows, and familiar with suffering" or, as the King James Version puts it, "acquainted with grief" (Isaiah 53:3). God knows sorrow. He knows suffering. He knows grief.

Nicholas Wolterstorff points out that God did not eliminate suffering with "some mighty blow of power," though he certainly could have. No, God "sent his beloved son to suffer *like* us, through his suffering to redeem us from suffering and evil. Instead of explaining our suffering God shares it."[8]

So God can and does share in our suffering. This does not diminish God but provides a more complete portrait of who he is. God is not threatened by emotion but is big enough to encompass emotions of all kinds. His ability to feel and experience suffering is confirmed ultimately in the crucifixion of Jesus. On the cross Jesus experienced the physical agony of human torture and death as well as the existential agony of the sin and guilt of the world. Because Jesus took on our pain and suffering, we have a God who understands human suffering.

In fact God's capacity to suffer is essential if we are to believe that God is a God of love. Moltmann says, "If God were in every way incapable of suffering, he would also be incapable of love."[9] Because God is love, he suffers. "God does not suffer out of deficiency of being," as we human beings do. "But he does suffer from his love, which is the overflowing superabundance of his being."[10] Because God loves our loved ones even more than we do, he grieves and suffers when their lives are cut short, when tragedy overtakes them and us.

"God is love. That is why he suffers," writes Wolterstorff. "The one who does not see God's suffering does not see his love. God is suffering love."[11]

The God Who Is Present in Pain

The LORD is close to the brokenhearted
and saves those who are crushed in spirit. (Psalm 34:18)

If there is a God, then why didn't he prevent the suicide? Did God cause our suffering? The short answer is that we must appeal to free will. Christians have long held that God honors our actions, even self-destructive ones. God does not prevent us from smoking cigarettes even though it could lead to lung cancer; nor does he prevent us from getting ourselves drunk and causing a car accident. God gives us freedom to make our own choices, even when they are bad ones. "For God to grant human beings free will was to grant us the awful dignity of making real choices with real consequences."[12] When our loved ones killed themselves, they were exercising their free will. Though God is grieved by their suicides, God honored their freedom to make that decision, tragic and horrible though it is.

The problem of pain and suffering cannot be "solved" by mere philosophical reasoning or speculation. It is not answered by glib clichés about hypothetical purposes or meanings behind the suffering. The solution is personal, not philosophical. The personal solution is that God himself experiences suffering through the person of Jesus. When words cannot comfort, the Word who became pierced flesh speaks to us out of his own pain and agony. Because he was betrayed, tortured and abandoned, God understands our feelings of betrayal, torture and abandonment. In Jesus, God approached humanity and took his stand with us. He suffered at the hands of the world just as we do.

Philosopher Peter Kreeft says, "God's answer to the problem of suffering is that he came right down into it. Many Christians try to get God off the hook for suffering; God put himself on the hook, so to speak—on the cross."[13]

One of my favorite writers is the British biblical scholar John Stott. In his magnum opus *The Cross of Christ* he probes the relationship between human suffering and the cross. Stott notes that while the cross is symbolic of such concepts as perseverance and service, the most profound meaning of the cross is the pain of God. "The cross of Christ is the proof of God's solidary love," Stott writes, "that is, of his personal, loving solidarity with us in our pain." God is not oblivious to our cries of suffering. "We are not to envisage him on a deck-chair, but on a cross. The God who allows us to suffer, once suffered himself in Christ, and continues to suffer with us and for us today."[14]

Stott finds helpful the work of Japanese theologian Kazoh Kitamori, who wrote *The Theology of the Pain of God* shortly after World War II.

Kitamori sees the pain of God as the heart of the Christian gospel, revealed in the cross. God's pain "results from the love of the One who intercepts and blocks his wrath towards us, the One who himself is smitten by his wrath."[15] God the Father suffers pain because of the death of his Son, Jesus, on the cross. This is analogous to the Japanese concept of *tsurasa,* "which consists of the suffering of the one who, in order to save the others whom he loves, inflicts pain upon himself or upon his son, even going so far as to put him to death."[16] Jesus' willingness to suffer and die on behalf of fallen humanity is the agonizing, ultimate fulfillment of God's loving pain and painful love.

"I could never myself believe in God, if it were not for the cross," concludes Stott. "In the real world of pain, how could one worship a God who was immune to it?" The God worthy of worship is not some impassive smiling Buddha but the bleeding man on the cross. "That is the God for me! He laid aside his immunity to pain. He entered our world of flesh and blood, tears and death. He suffered for us. Our sufferings become more manageable in light of his."[17]

Therefore human suffering does not mean that God is absent or uncaring. The only possible solution to the suffering of humanity is that God exists and has taken suffering upon himself. As the hymn "Crown Him with Many Crowns" says:

Crown him the Son of God
Before the worlds began,
And ye, who tread where he hath trod
Crown him the Son of Man,
Who every grief has known
That wrings the human breast
And takes and bears them for his own
That all in him may rest.[18]

Jesus is the One who has known every grief. Every loss, every trauma that wrings the human breast, Jesus has taken upon himself and bears as his own. Jesus is the only person who can authentically say he knows our every grief.

He has "borne our griefs and carried our sorrows" (Isaiah 53:4 RSV). Why? So that we may find rest in him. He invites us to come to him, we who are weary and heavy-laden, so that he can give us rest. Through his stripes, we are healed.

Not only does God suffer because he identifies with humanity as a whole, he also suffers because he identifies with the church. Paul writes that all those who follow Jesus Christ are members of the body of Christ. "Now you are the body of Christ, and each one of you is a part of it" (1 Corinthians 12:27). If we are part of the church, we are part of Christ's body. If we suffer as part of the church, Christ himself suffers. If his body suffers pain and grief, God suffers pain and grief.

So where is God when it hurts? If we are part of the human race, he is present with us in our suffering because God identifies with the suffering of all humanity through Jesus' incarnation. And if we are Christians, he is present in our suffering because God identifies with the suffering of those who are part of the body of Christ.

Even those who cannot bring themselves to fully believe in God after a suicide find themselves terrified of the alternative. A universe without God would be even worse than a painful one where God is with us in our pain, for we would be utterly alone in our suffering. One griever wrote that "alone" is "the belief that there is no higher order, only random acts of cruelty or coincidental acts of kindness. It is hell."[19]

C. S. Lewis concluded that God's seeming absence during grief is simply because of the traumatic nature of grief. "The time when there is nothing at all in your soul except a cry for help may be just the time when God can't give it: you are like the drowning man who can't be helped because he clutches and grabs. Perhaps your own reiterated cries deafen you to the voice you hoped to hear."[20]

On a human level, we often realize the significance of a relationship when a person is farthest away from us. Lovers long for one another when they are parted; parents become acutely aware of their love for their college-age children when the nest is empty. Perhaps this helps us understand why we cry out for God when we feel abandoned by him. Henri Nouwen writes, "The mystery of God's presence, therefore, can be touched only by a deep awareness of his absence. It is in the center of our longing for the absent God that we discover his footprints."[21]

The Bible suggests that, paradoxically, God's seeming absence can actually indicate his presence. The Gospel of Luke is bookended by two parallel narratives. At the beginning of the Gospel, Luke tells the story of a Passover feast where two pilgrims, Mary and Joseph, go to Jerusalem with their son, Jesus. After the feast is over, Mary and Joseph make their way back to their hometown Nazareth, not realizing that Jesus has stayed behind in Jerusalem. Only later do they realize that he is missing, and they return to Jerusalem to find him on the third day.

Then, at the end of the same Gospel, Luke tells another story. Another Passover feast has taken place in Jerusalem, and two pilgrims are walking to their hometown, Emmaus. They are grieving because their teacher, Jesus of Nazareth, has been executed. On their way home they meet a stranger and discuss with him the events of the past week. The two disciples, probably a husband and wife, invite this stranger into their home for a meal. As the guest breaks bread with them, they recognize that this man is none other than Jesus himself. Their rediscovery of Jesus' identity takes place on the third day.[22]

The literary parallelism between the two stories is intentional. In the first Passover story, the pilgrims think Jesus is with them, but he's not. In the second case, they think Jesus *isn't* with them, but he really *is*. The pastoral lesson for us is that sometimes, when times are good, we get caught up in everyday life and don't notice if God is there or not. But at times of loss and tragedy, when we experience grief, we think God is absent. We think he's no longer there, he doesn't care for us, we're on our own. Our downcast eyes cannot see the God who walks beside us.

Where is God when it hurts? He is with us when life seems darkest, when we feel most hopeless, when he seems most distant. At these times God draws closest to us in unexpected and mysterious ways. Our grief journey may be much like that of the disciples on the road to Emmaus. In our grief and loss, Jesus comes alongside us. He is not intrusive, but he is available to break bread with us and rekindle our hope.

Part III

Life After Suicide

The paradox is indeed that new life is born out of the pains of the old.
HENRI NOUWEN

9

The *Spirituality* of Grief

This is the paradox of our faith: joy is forged in sorrow.
And death leads to life. And grief is the road between them.
WALTER WANGERIN

*B*ruce was in college when his cousin killed himself by shooting himself in the head. "It was a total shock when he did this," Bruce said, "because Jason had been a Christian." In fact Jason had been the first person to introduce Bruce to the person of Jesus.

Bruce was a philosophy minor at the time, and all of his courses were teaching him that life had no purpose. Contrary to his studies, Bruce decided, "There has to be some reason for living. There has to be some ultimate purpose, some ultimate hope. And I'm going to find out what it is."

In the months following his cousin's suicide, Bruce embarked on a quest for the truth. "Even though Jason had introduced me to the Christian faith, I had never embraced it for myself," Bruce remembers. He went to a Christian event, where he bought a copy of *Mere Christianity* by C. S. Lewis. He read that book and the Gospel of John, met

Christian peers, and eventually came face to face with the reality of Christianity. "That's it," Bruce concluded. "That's the missing piece." In finding Christ, he also found peace.

"My cousin's suicide was a defining moment in my life," Bruce says. It was the crisis that jolted him to look for God and led him to faith in Jesus Christ.

Walter Wangerin says that grief is a process that turns the bereaved back to life. "The goodness of their grieving is that it brings them by stages into the stream of the living again, however slowly, however painfully."[1] We do not stand by the grave forever. If we grieve properly, grief moves us back to life as different, changed people.

Just as grief can bring us back to living, says Wangerin, it can also turn us toward God. Those separated from their loved ones can be drawn back to God's love and eternal life. If grief helps us face life on this earth, it also can help us live forever in eternity. While grief drives some away from God, it can also drive us toward him.

While some claim that suffering and tragedy are evidences of God's nonexistence or lack of care for us, for many others God is more present and sensed with a greater reality in times of great pain. Many people who would otherwise never give thought to spiritual issues come face to face with God in grief or loss. We experience God's grace and comfort in times of tragedy. Grief, far from being an experience that alienates us from God, can prompt us to apprehend deeper spiritual realities.

Many Christians throughout church history have spoken of the spirituality of grief. Personal pain has a sacramental aspect. If we never experience pain, then we will never experience comfort, for we do not need it. But if we are pierced with heartrending agony, that pain can drive us to the One whose hands and feet were also pierced.

The shortest verse of the Bible, "Jesus wept," tells us that Jesus was not so far removed from humanity that he could not share our pain. In his tears for Lazarus, Jesus showed us that he cares about us, that he feels what we feel, that our hurt is his hurt, that our grief is his as well. The God of the Bible, the God we meet through Jesus, is the God who weeps with us. When we come to Christ, we are inseparably united to him, and we become part of his body. When one part of the body mourns, the whole body mourns together. Our grief helps us see that Christ himself cries with our tears.

We would find no comfort in God unless he himself were capable of feeling pain. And we would not truly experience God's comfort without pain to be comforted. Having experienced grief himself, God understands our grief. And through our grief, we understand God.

Is There a Purpose for Suffering?

Suffering purifies us, the questions that pour forth define us. Our unknowing makes us pace the floor at night, alternately shaking our fist at God and begging him to hold us close, to tell us everything will be all right, that someday it will all make sense. We scream as the flames lick us, begging for mercy. Are you there, God? Why is this happening?[2]

One common response to pain and suffering is to search for a reason behind it. When evil strikes, when tragedy occurs, Christians often wonder why such things happen. We assume that there must always be a reason. But Christians in the New Testament do not spend a lot of time pondering *why* misfortune or persecution occur. Rather than looking for philosophical answers to the mysteries of pain and suffering, the early Christians simply saw evil as a fact of life. For them, suffering was part of living in a fallen, imperfect world. They did not try to *understand* evil; rather, they *opposed* it. Pain and suffering come from evil spiritual beings and forces, not some mysterious good purposes of God.[3]

Furthermore, modern Christians in the industrialized world tend to assume that "normal" means a life without pain, grief, loss or suffering. As one commentator observes, "Some modern presentations of the gospel leave little room for suffering as an aspect of the Christian life." Western Christians are conditioned to "regard most suffering as an intrusion on the tranquil life that they feel is their God-given due."[4] Pain is seen as a problem to be fixed. When we have a head-ache, we take a pain reliever. When we are sick, we go to the doctor and get an antibiotic. The relative ease with which we eliminate many physical hurts lulls us into believing that pain is merely a temporary blip until we can find a quick cure.

But most people throughout human history would consider this an unheard-of state of affairs. In centuries past and around the globe yet today, millions of people live and die without the expectation of eas-ily accessible medical care. Disease, famine and poverty are the default position. If you lack clean water or adequate food on a daily basis, suffering is not an aberration to be quickly remedied. Because death is no stranger, suffering is simply taken for granted.

Those of us who live a sanitized existence amid sophisticated tech-nology see death and affliction as unusual, so we wrestle with the "why" questions. Those in less affluent situations see death and afflic-tion as normal. In a book about the global persecution of Christians, Paul Marshall points out that many American Christian books on self-esteem and inner peace are completely irrelevant to Christians who are being tortured, raped and murdered.[5] Rather than wondering, "Why is this happening? Why are we suffering?" persecuted Christians are keenly aware of the reality (and normality) of evil. They are also far more conscious that Christian hope and deliverance transcend the mere elimination of affliction or pain.

Missionary Ruth Padilla Eldrenkamp, whose husband was mur-dered by car thieves on an isolated road in the Andes, said, "I must remind myself and others that this is the kind of world we live in: a broken world, full of emptiness, wracked by injustice and consequent poverty and violence. The question, then, is not 'Why?' but 'Why not?' Why should we as Christians expect immunity from pain and loss while most of the world suffers them?"[6]

Because we live in a fallen world, we should expect pain and suf-fering. Good and evil are at war, and we are sometimes casualties of the crossfire. "Suffering is not expected in paradise but *is* expected in a state of war. The logical 'problem of evil' disappears for us when we accept the warfare worldview of the Bible."[7]

We shouldn't assume that our sufferings are instigated by God. More likely they are simply the result of living in an imperfect world. Things are not the way God intended them to be. We live in a world where cars crash and health fails. This is not God's design. This world is in decay and corruption, and it will not be fully renewed and restored until the complete advent of the kingdom of God.

C. S. Lewis's grief led him to struggle with the possibility that "there is nothing we can do with suffering except to suffer it."[8] Perhaps this points to what is wrongheaded about our attempts to escape suffering. Perhaps at times suffering is simply to be suffered. There may be no other way through it.

So what are the implications of all this? Suffering is normative, not exceptional. Rather than trying to intellectually *understand* suffering and the problem of evil, we *act* in response to it. Let's not waste our time pondering unfathomable mysteries; we simply must do what we can to bring relief. If there is suffering in the world, we act to relieve it. When we see disease and injury, we work to bring healing and recovery. When we encounter famine, we feed the hungry. When we see injustice and oppression, we expose it and denounce it.

And when we experience grief and loss, we offer comfort. Jesus' mission was to bind up the brokenhearted and to comfort all who mourn (Isaiah 61:1-2; Luke 4:17-21). Those of us who are his followers are called to do likewise.

God is already at work to comfort the bereaved, to protect the orphan and widow, to defend the oppressed. When we participate in these kinds of activities, we join with God in his work of relieving suffering and opposing evil.

God's suffering gives us the opportunity to rest in his divine nature. Because he has suffered, we can come to him knowing that he understands our loss. He is not some cold, aloof God who shrugs when we mourn. He is larger than the grief and pain, but he is not distant from it. God has borne unimaginable grief and suffering, the cumulative sufferings of all of humanity, the countless victims of genocide and torture and unknown holocausts. While our minds reel, simply incapable of understanding such agony, God grieves and suffers far more fully than any of us can know or imagine.

Because God is the ultimate sufferer, he is the ultimate One to whom we can turn when we suffer. Because he has borne the grief of millions, he can bear our grief as well. He can handle our anger, our rage, our shame, our guilt. He will hear our cries, he will hold us in our weeping, he will listen to our questions. And ultimately he will wipe away our tears. He may not necessarily take away our grief or our pain, not right away. The suffering may linger with us just as it lingers with him. But when we shed tears, he will envelop us in his all-consuming love and remind us that he also grieves and mourns. When we shed our tears, God sheds tears as well.

God doesn't only absorb the pain of grief and loss; he makes a way through it. Because suffering is within the realm of God's comprehension and knowledge, it becomes a point of contact between us and God. If God knows suffering and we know suffering, then we can know God even in the midst of the suffering. God can be known through suffering because he has made himself available to us through it, through opening himself up to the pain and grief of this world.

That's the bottom line for those of us who ask the why questions about the suicide of a loved one. We cannot ultimately understand why something happened. We should not think that God has some mysterious divine purpose for our suffering. Neither should we think that our experience of suffering and loss means that God has abandoned us. On the contrary, as John Stott has written, "God's pledge is not that suffering will never afflict us, but that it will never separate us from his love."[9]

From Despair to Hope

The most autobiographical of all of the apostle Paul's writings is probably his second letter to the Corinthians. With candid honesty and vulnerability, Paul discusses his own suffering and despair. During a time of great hardship in Paul's ministry, he says, "we were under great pressure, far beyond our ability to endure, so that we despaired even of life. Indeed, in our hearts we felt the sentence of death" (2 Corinthians 1:8-9). Later on in the same letter, Paul writes:

> Five times I received from the Jews the forty lashes minus one. Three times I was beaten with rods, once I was stoned, three times I was shipwrecked, I spent a night and a day in the open sea, I have been constantly on the move. I have been in danger from rivers, in danger from bandits, in danger from my own countrymen, in danger from Gentiles; in danger in the city, in danger in the country, in danger at sea; and in danger from false brothers. I have labored and toiled and have often gone without sleep; I have known hunger and thirst and have often gone without food; I have been cold and naked. (2 Corinthians 11:24-27)

No wonder Paul despaired of life! What gave him the courage to go on? Why did he not give in to despair? What hope did he cling to?

Paul saw that because he was undergoing suffering, he would be better able to comfort others who were experiencing similar suffering. One theologian says, "Christians do not merely tolerate suffering; rather, through it they share in each other's experience."[10] As Paul writes in his blessing at the beginning of 2 Corinthians,

> Praise be to the God and Father of our Lord Jesus Christ, the Father of compassion and the God of all comfort, who comforts us in all our troubles, so that we can comfort those in any trouble with the comfort we ourselves have received from God. For just as the sufferings of Christ flow over into our lives, so also through Christ our comfort over-flows. . . . Our hope for you is firm, because we know that just as you share in our sufferings, so also you share in our comfort. (2 Corinthians 1:3-5, 7)

Here we see a pattern of cause and effect. Jesus himself experienced suffering. Because he suffered, he knows what we go through when we experience suffering. Therefore he is able to comfort us. We are able to receive comfort from Jesus because he understands suffering and pain. He knows the anguish of pain and tragic death. Jesus offers no pat answers for our grief and suffering. No, Jesus stands with us and says, "I too have entered the depths of human suffering." His identification with us tells us that we are not alone. I am not the only person to walk this path. Jesus has walked this way before me.

Therefore our own suffering and grief are no longer meaningless. Our suffering brings us into communion with Jesus. While God does not cause our suffering, through it we gain understanding of the suffering of Jesus. Though Jesus is the One who heals, he is also the One who is wounded, broken, tortured and crucified. Jesus went through unbearable agony, excruciating suffering, horrible abandonment and betrayal. We must fight the temptation to turn away from these pictures of Jesus in agony. Because it is this Jesus, with bloody brow and pierced hands and feet, who whispers to us, "I know how you feel. I know the pain, the agony you are going through. You are not alone in this. I am not some impassive God who doesn't care. I am the suffering God who understands."

Furthermore, our suffering brings us into relationship with others who suffer. Before our loss, we may not have known what to do or say to those who have experienced loss. But now we know how it feels. For we have been there. We walk the same path. We can bring comfort to others who are experiencing similar pain.

The late spiritual writer Henri Nouwen says that grief is the pathway to compassion. "Grief asks me to allow the sins of the world—my own included—to pierce my heart and make me shed tears, many tears, for them. There is no compassion without many tears."[11]

President Abraham Lincoln was no stranger to grief. In 1850 the Lincolns spent fifty-two days at the bedside of their three-year-old son, Eddie, before losing him to tuberculosis. Then in the second year of his presidency, they lost their eleven-year-old Willie to typhoid fever. Lincoln's wife, Mary, was devastated by these losses. But the loss of his sons perhaps prepared Lincoln to preside during the Civil War. "Lincoln would somehow find the strength to merge his own grief with the grief of his countrymen."[12]

"Grief allows me to see beyond my wall and realize the immense suffering that results from human lostness," writes Nouwen. "It opens my heart to a genuine solidarity with other humans."[13]

So suffering moves us out of despair toward comfort. It points us toward eternal truths, as Ken Gire notes: "Suffering sensitizes us not only to the world around us, which is needy, but to the world within us, which is needier still, and ultimately to the world beyond us, which we long for in so many ways. Yet in so few ways do we ever fully realize it. Until we suffer." Our suffering points us to the suffering of Jesus. Once we understand this, "then the road ahead, however long, however difficult, is infinitely easier to travel."[14]

Until eternity, we live with the imperfect and suffer the consequences. Good things can come out of our pain, even if only our realization of our dependence on God.

Paul writes in 2 Corinthians 4:8-9, "We are hard pressed on every side, but not crushed; perplexed but not in despair; persecuted, but not abandoned; struck down, but not destroyed." His change in tone here is striking. Just a little earlier he was despairing of life. How can he now say that he was perplexed but not in despair? Why this change of perspective?

He goes on: "Therefore we do not lose heart. Though outwardly we are wasting away, yet inwardly we are being renewed day by day. For our light and momentary troubles are achieving for us an eternal glory that far outweighs them all" (2 Corinthians 4:16-17).

I wish my father could have understood this. Even though his physical body was wasting away, his inner self could have been renewed day by day. Even though the physical deterioration and suffering were awful, in reality they were nothing compared to the eternal glory that far outweighs any suffering on this earth! Our loved ones were overwhelmed by their suffering; they could not see that their suffering could have been overwhelmed by an eternal glory that would far outweigh the pain.

What Paul points to in 2 Corinthians is that even in the midst of pain and suffering, we can look to the hope of glory. Those of us left behind by our loved ones must not allow our grief and suffering to bring us to despair. Our choice is between despair and hope. We can have the same hope that Paul had, that Jesus had, that these sufferings are only temporary. If we give in to despair, then we continue the cycle and death wins. If we cling to hope, life triumphs over death.

Most people use *hope* as a verb: "I hope things will turn out better" or "I hoped he wouldn't do this." When *hope* is a verb, it is usually just wishful thinking on our part. We crank up our feelings and try to generate enough emotional or mental energy to bring something into reality. Such hope is only a human activity, limited by our finitude.

But the Bible uses *hope* as a noun. "For most people, hoping is something that they *do,* but the Bible talks about hope as something they can *possess.*"[15] Hope, in the Christian sense of the word, is far more than a wish or a dream. It's a tangible thing, as real as any object. *"We have this hope* as an anchor for the soul, firm and secure" (Hebrews 6:19). Our hope is a noun, as solid as a cast-iron anchor. And that hope is the hope of resurrection.

We do not merely hope for resurrection; we affirm the fact that Jesus rose from the dead. This historical event is our anchor. Because Jesus rose from the dead, so will we. Because Jesus arose from suffering and death, we can too. We participate in his resurrection. We cling to his resurrected body, and we anchor ourselves to that resurrection hope.

Reinterpreting Our Loss

Four months after my father's death, I heard a news story on the radio about a new medical treatment that transplants nerves into the brains of stroke victims. That triggered an idea that I had not previously considered: What if my father had simply died of the stroke in November rather than the suicide in February?

If that initial stroke had killed him, his death would not have brought the troublesome questions unique to suicide. It would still have been very painful, but perhaps the death would have felt more understandable because it was a "natural" one. It would not have had the stigma of suicide, and explaining Dad's death to others would not have been quite as difficult.

However, if he had died in November, it would have come as an utter shock, with no warning whatsoever. I would have felt an even greater sense of unfinished business, with many more things left unsaid. But because he survived the stroke and lived for three more months before his suicide, I was able to communicate with my dad in important ways prior to his death. During those three months I saw my father's humanity and vulnerability as I never had before. I connected with him and communicated with him with greater authenticity and transparency. The stroke had not killed him, but it enabled him to face his mortality; out of that we were able to have some significant conversations that I will always remember. Also, the fact that he survived the stroke alerted my dad to his physical limitations and helped him seek spiritual meaning and faith.

So though the stroke ultimately led to his debilitation, depression and suicide, I am grateful for those three months of life. They were terrible months for my father, so bad that he ultimately despaired of life. But they were a mixed blessing. Even though I wish my father had not chosen suicide, in some ways his suicide in February was better than a death by stroke in November. Somehow the whole experience brought him to reconciliation with God.

Many suicide survivors in other circumstances may not be able to find any redemptive value in their loved one's death. Maybe in the majority of cases it is impossible to find any "benefit" or "greater good" in a person's suicide. I do not want to make trite remarks about reasons behind how things happen, because maybe there aren't any, and it's naive to attempt to find a satisfactory justification for what happened. But in this particular situation, it was helpful to realize what I would not have experienced had my dad died of more natural circumstances three months earlier. That understanding was another step in finding peace.

Never Closure, Always Healing

"I can't handle the word 'closure.' I get sick of hearing it. The first time someone asked me about closure was the day after Julie's burial.

Of course I was still in hell then. In a way, I still am. How can there ever be true closure? A part of my heart is gone."[16]

When I was in elementary school, I had a habit of making sure that the last thing I said to my parents each night was "Good night," and I expected them to respond likewise. I became agitated if they would respond with other words, or if they said any additional phrases or sentences after saying good night. I was worried that they or I would die during the night and that our final words to each other would not have closure. Even as a child, I was aware of the importance of ending conversations well.

For that reason, I am grateful for the final phone conversation I had with my dad a few weeks before he died. Even though he was in the midst of depression, his thinking was still clear enough that he could tell me he appreciated me and was proud of me. Most suicide survivors do not have that opportunity to share last words, or they only do so at the casket or the gravesite. Suicides usually leave unfinished conversations filled with loose ends.

But ultimate closure is an unrealistic expectation. We can close on a house, but we can't close on a person's life. To put the past behind us and lock it up into a little box dishonors the memory of our loved one; it says that we are trying to pretend that this didn't happen. It's a form of denial. No, instead we acknowledge what happened, and that it was tragic; we acknowledge that it has changed our lives forever. We live on as changed people who look at life and death differently now.

Eventually we come to the point of realizing that though we may always grieve we no longer do so continually or consciously. In some ways grief will go on forever. In other ways it does come to some end points. After his wife's death, C. S. Lewis wrote *A Grief Observed* in a series of four notebooks. He decided that he would not buy any new notebooks after the fourth one. He said, "I thought I could describe a *state,* make a map of sorrow. Sorrow, however, turns out to be not a state but a process. It needs not a map but a history, and if I don't stop writing that history at some quite arbitrary point, there's no reason why I should ever stop. There is something new to be chronicled every day."[17]

Two days after my father's funeral, Ellen and I flew to California for a conference for Asian Americans in our organization. I wasn't sure that I was ready to be there, but it was an opportunity to get some distance from the events of the past week and find time for processing. The first night of the conference, during a time of singing, one of the worship songs was a prayer for God to "hold me close," to let his love surround me. I was able to come to God with all my brokenness, grief and pain and have a sense of his presence, comfort and love. It was the beginning of the healing process. I did not find "closure," but I experienced God's *closeness*.

Healing doesn't mean that we are ever completely "recovered." We are never fully "healed." The human body is never in a state of perfect health; it is constantly in flux, with some cells dying while others are growing. Every day we experience hundreds of minuscule injuries, paper cuts and abrasions and nicks, and if our bodies are healthy, they are always in the process of healing. It is better to speak of experiencing *healing* as an ongoing process than to pretend we have been *healed* and have arrived at a final destination.

Another way of looking at it is that our initial grief is like an open wound. Over time, with care and restoration, the wound closes, but it remains tender, painful. It doesn't take much to hurt it again. Bump it just a little, jostle it too much, and the wound may open up again and need more care and bandaging. But eventually it will heal enough that it is not as painful to touch. It may still be sensitive, the area may bruise easily, but the excruciating pain has subsided.

Grief "is a natural, spontaneous *process* of healing. Even as a broken bone—by no thought of our own but by the nature of bones— commences to mend, so the soul broken by death starts step by step to heal."[18] Grieving and the healing of grief are gradual processes. Lewis likens the process to "the warming of a room or the coming of daylight. When you first notice them they have already been going for some time."[19]

We are never completely healed. After all, we still carry the scars. But grief that has done its work in us will help us experience God's grace more fully.

God has always been a God of paradox and reversal. The last shall be first. Death comes out of life. Our encounter with suicide and despair can lead us to comfort and hope.

10

The Healing

Community

*In community, our fears and anger are transformed
by God's unconditional love. . . . In community . . . God's
compassion becomes present in the midst of a broken world.*
HENRI NOUWEN

*T*he brochure showed up anonymously in my mail slot at work.
"Survivors of Suicide is a support group open to anyone who has experienced the loss of a relative or friend through suicide," it read. "Survivors need a safe place to explore their feelings of grief and anger, to raise questions and doubts. We will welcome you at any time."

Six months had passed since my father's death, and I thought I was holding together well enough. Did I need to attend a support group? I wasn't sure. The flyer sat on my desk for weeks until I finally told myself that I would check it out. Maybe it would help me in ways I could not yet anticipate.

The session began with a reading of the serenity prayer. Over cookies and juice, members of the group took turns telling stories of what had happened to their loved ones. A sister who had slit her wrists. A fiancé who had hung himself. Boxes of tissues were passed around as tears flowed.

When it was my turn, I choked up as I told the group my story. I had not cried for my father for some months now, and I was surprised that tears came back so quickly. As heads nodded around the room, I exhaled a long-pent-up breath of relief. These were people who understood the grief of suicide. I didn't have to worry about what they would think of me or the suicide; they were a community of fellow survivors, helping one another grieve on the journey.

Whether or not you have access to a suicide survivors support group, we all need to be part of some sort of community to help us find healing. Healing rarely comes in isolation. We may be tempted to retreat from the world and hide in our pain, but when we draw on the resources of those around us, we will find that we are not alone in our grief. Even if others have not known the specific loss of a suicide, they can provide comfort to us and ease our burden.

We need to be open to the healing that comes from relationship. All human beings were created with two distinct relational needs: we are designed to be in relationship with God and in relationship with other people. Another way of looking at it is that we all have a God-shaped hole and a people-shaped hole. This is why Jesus taught that the greatest commandments are to love the Lord your God and to love your neighbor as yourself. Relationship with God fills the God-shaped hole, and relationships with others fill the people-shaped hole.

Following a tragedy, our soul feels as if it is full of holes. There is a hollow emptiness in our chest, an inner ache of pain and loss. To find healing and restoration, we need to fill that empty hole with both love from God and love from others. We do so through the parallel spiritual disciplines of solitude and community. In solitude we draw near to God and receive his comfort, grace and reassurance. In community we build relationships with other people who can provide tangible support and kindness.

We need both kinds of love to bring us back to wholeness and health. If we look only to God as our source for restoration, we will withdraw from people and nurture a private, inward-looking grief, which is not healthy. God created us to be in relationship with other people. Likewise, our relationships with people are most helpful when they point us to God. While there is great benefit in talking about our experiences and feelings, we also need spiritual content, time shared in prayer for one another and in Scripture and other spiritual resources. Otherwise we are merely relying on ourselves rather than turning to the power and comfort of God.

So we must open ourselves to the care and nurture of friends, family, church members, others who can watch over us and help us. This can make us feel vulnerable, as it exposes us to the potential of reopening wounds of grief. But taking the risk opens us to healing for ourselves, as well as making a difference in other people's lives.

Just as the human body has the ability and capacity to heal its own wounds, so too the body of Christ can heal itself when one part is injured. A body part does not heal on its own power, in isolation from the rest of the body. It depends on nutrients being digested and carried through the bloodstream, antibodies that ward off infection, and continued health of the overall body to protect the wounded area while it is healing.

So it is with the body of Christ. In the community of the church, healing comes when other parts of the body join together to bring the wounded parts the resources needed for recovery. Some people serve as antibodies, warding off things that might cause further pain. Others are blood cells bringing oxygen and life to the wounded parts and taking away the garbage. The body of Christ has the life of Christ dwelling within it. While we each draw life and hope from God as individuals, we also experience the healing and recovery that come from being a part of his body. God is the source of life, and that life-giving, healing Spirit is experienced most fully when we are living in relationship with other parts of the body of Christ.

How Friends and Family Can Help

During my sophomore year of high school I was smitten with a girl in my class; some of our mutual friends told me I was rather obsessed with her. When she told me she was not interested in dating, I spun into a season of gloom and depression. I was constantly downcast and listless. Life felt meaningless.

As a member of my school's debate team, I attended a two-week summer debate camp at a local college. My friend Dan, my roommate that week, tells me that I alternated between extremes of bouncing-off-the-walls hyperactivity and down-in-the-dumps despondency. I browsed the college library and looked at books about suicide. This and my bipolar mood swings alarmed Dan, who challenged me and asked me how I was doing. Months later I learned that camp counselors had put me on suicide watch.

While I never made an actual suicide attempt, this teenage flirtation with suicidal thinking lingers in my memory. When I read news reports of teen suicides, I wonder if that could have been me, had I been allowed to sink deeper into my melancholy. I am grateful for Dan and others whose friendship kept me alive.

Years later, Dan was one of the first people I called after I found out about my dad's death, and I asked him for his prayers. A few months after my father's funeral, Dan called me to say, "Al, I feel like I need to apologize to you."

"Why?" I asked.

"Because I don't think I've been a very good friend to you," he said. He had wanted to help me but hadn't known what to say or do, so he didn't do anything. "I should have at least sent a card," Dan said.

"That's okay," I replied, grateful for Dan's honesty. I was glad to hear that he hadn't been blindly ignoring me. He needed to hear from me that I understood his awkwardness in expressing comfort.

Suicide is bewildering enough for the immediate survivors; those surrounding the survivors are often even more at a loss for what to say and do. My wife told me later that she had no idea what to do to get me through it. We had been married for only a few months, and the newlywed instruction manual didn't say anything about what to do in the case of parental suicide. The best thing she did for me was simply to be there beside me. I didn't need her to give me counseling; I just needed her companionship.

What can friends of survivors of suicide do for them? Pray. Listen. Send cards. Provide company. Help with practical details, funeral arrangements, food, phone calls and so on. If you don't know what to do, far better simply to say "I don't really know what to do or say" than to not do or say anything at all. That simple admission itself communicates care and concern. In some small way, the fact that others are at a loss about what to do provides a point of identification with suicide survivors who may feel completely at a loss.

Survivors of suicide don't need pat answers to incomprehensible questions. We simply need the loving presence of others to help us keep our lives going. We need companions on the journey, not answers. We don't need the pain to be minimized; we want others to be willing to be with us in our pain and grief. Nicholas Wolterstorff says, "I need to hear from you that you are with me in my desperation. To comfort me, you have to come close. Come sit beside me on my mourning bench."[1]

Consolation can seem woefully empty at times. Well-intentioned people may attempt to comfort, but their words often seem meaningless. Their actions may end up being more hurtful than helpful, like the words of Job's friends when they told him that his calamities were the result of his sin. "Miserable comforters are you all!" Job lashed out. "Will your long-winded speeches never end?" (Job 16:2-3).

When people die, the bereaved are often assailed by such pious clichés as "God took him home" or "God decided it was his time to go." Even in cases of natural death these kinds of statements are rarely helpful, since the survivors then feel as if God is responsible for the death. In the case of suicide, they are even more disturbing since they are tantamount to saying that God killed our loved one or induced her to kill herself. That is not the portrait of the biblical God. The truth is that our loved one chose the suicide. To say any more goes beyond what can be humanly known.

One of my relatives, in an effort to be encouraging, trotted out the cliché "God doesn't give us anything we can't handle. What doesn't kill you makes you stronger." My reaction to this was anger. What did she mean? What are the implications of this? According to this kind of thinking, my dad wasn't strong enough to handle what God had given him, so it killed him. She intended to tell me to buck up and be strong, but instead I heard her imply that my father was weak, that he took his own life because he wasn't strong enough to handle his debilitation.

Another nonhelpful platitude is "All things work together for good." This reference to Romans 8:28, while meant to comfort, minimizes the reality of tragic loss. It is often misused, implying that awful, horrible events should be seen as hidden blessings. This is a misapplication of this verse. A more accurate translation of the verse reads, "In all things God works for the good of those who love him." In other words, abstract "things" do not work together for good; *God* is the active agent at work. The events in our lives may or may not be good. In fact they often are very bad. But God remains good, and he is capable of bringing good out of painful situations.

As Wolterstorff says, "But please: Don't say it's not really so bad. Because it is. Death is awful, demonic. If you think your task as comforter is to tell me that really, all things considered, it's not so bad, you do not sit with me in my grief but place yourself off in the distance away from me. Over there, you are of no help."[2]

As time passes, some things get easier while others stay the same. Sometimes someone will ask me if I'm okay, and I'll sigh and say, "I don't know. I suppose." Other times people will ask about how my mother or brother is doing, and I'll wonder, *How am I supposed to know? I don't even know how I feel, let alone anyone else.*

While we need comfort from friends and relatives, "sometimes we reject comfort because our grief is too raw, our pain too overwhelming."[3] We need to be patient with them, and they need to be patient with us. Grief is not easy for any of us, and it may take some time for us to come to the point where we are able to open up to others.

"And later, when you ask me how I am doing and I respond with a quick, thoughtless 'Fine' or 'OK,' stop me sometime and ask, 'No, I mean *really*.'"

How to Talk About Suicide

Some time after my father's suicide, my pastor, Matthew, told me about an illustration he had omitted from a recent sermon. It was a joke about a man talking to someone on the ledge of a building, trying to talk him out of jumping, with the punch line being that both men jump off.

Matthew told me, "The more I thought about it, I realized that that wasn't really very funny. I said to myself, *Al wouldn't think that was funny. Other church members who lost loved ones to suicide wouldn't find it funny.*" So Matthew decided not to use it and found another way to introduce his sermon.

I thanked him for his sensitivity. Matthew had demonstrated care and concern for suicide survivors by not treating suicide in a trivial way.

Survivors are hypersensitive to the topic of suicide. It punches us in the gut if someone jokes, "If this doesn't work out, I'm going to kill myself!" One survivor told me that she challenges coworkers who say things like that, asking them if they've ever considered how painful those flip comments might be to others. Suicide is no laughing matter.

How should people describe the act of suicide? This has been an ongoing debate for some years. The traditional phrase has been to say that someone "committed suicide." Survivors reacted against this, saying that it implies criminality, as one would commit murder. Is suicide a crime that is committed, like a burglary? In some cases, perhaps, but in many cases, no.

In the past few decades, psychologists and suicide survivor groups have moved toward saying that someone "completed suicide." In this parlance, suicide is not a single act but the final episode in what may have been a period of self-destructive tendencies.

The problem is that in many cases, suicide *is* a single act, not one of a series of attempts or part of a larger pattern. Furthermore, to say that someone "completed" suicide sounds like noting a laudatory accomplishment, like completing a term paper or college degree. It also comes across as somewhat clinical and cold.

So more recently, grief organizations and counselors have suggested that we use more neutral terms: for example, someone "died of suicide" or "died by suicide." The Compassionate Friends, an organization dedicated to helping families who have lost children, officially changed its language in 1999 so that all its materials reflect this. Executive director Diana Cunningham said, "Both expressions ['committed suicide' and 'completed suicide'] perpetuate a stigma that is neither accurate nor relevant to today's society."[5]

I resonate with this. I find it difficult to form the phrase "My dad committed suicide." And it seems wholly unnatural to say that "my dad completed suicide." It is somewhat easier to tell someone that "my dad died from suicide" or that "my dad took his own life."

I also recoil against descriptions of suicide attempts as "successful." If someone "succeeded" in killing himself, best to simply say that he killed himself after a series of attempts. There is no need to make a dreadful loss sound like a triumphant accomplishment. An "unsuccessful suicide attempt" is best described simply as a suicide attempt. Suicide survivor organizations have worked in recent years to help the media report on suicides with more neutral, sensitive language.

Preventing Other Suicides

Anchoring ourselves in community will also help us from slipping into despair and can prevent further suicides, whether our own or others'. Stephen Arterburn tells of a group counseling meeting at his Christian treatment center. At the end of the meeting, a boy stood up and asked for help, saying he was suicidal and had been visualizing putting a gun to his head. The boy sat down, and moments later a back door opened and a man with a turban and a hospital gown entered the room. He said, "If anyone here is thinking of killing yourself, I want to encourage you to reconsider. God loves you and wants you to live. This turban on my head is a bandage from where I put a gun to my head and pulled the trigger. Fortunately, I survived so I could come here and tell you not to do it. God loves you."[6]

If you find yourself falling into suicidal despair, heed the words of the man who walked into the group. He survived his attempt so that he could save the young man from the same fate. Learn from his mistake before you make your own. As Moses says in Deuteronomy 30:19, the choice of life or death is set before each of us. "Now choose life, so that you and your children may live."

Studies show that survivors of suicide are somewhat more likely than others to attempt suicide themselves. Research suggests that depression runs in families, and shared history and environment may lead family members to have similar temperamental tendencies. But this doesn't mean we are doomed to follow their example. The vast majority of survivors do not take their own lives. One survivor writes, "The suicide of a loved one can be a deterrent—or an antidote—to suicide and suicidal thoughts. In moments when I've thought about suicide, such thoughts are instantly followed by the thought, *Given what my father did, I could never do that to my family.*"[7]

Occasionally I am haunted by the possibility that my father's suicide makes me more vulnerable to suicide myself. I worry about genetic or hereditary tendencies that I may not know about, and I am besieged by random thoughts about what my own suicide might look like. When these thoughts occur to me during sleepless nights, I force myself to dismiss them from my mind. I think of my family and remind myself that I would never want to do to them what my father did to us. As an act of the will, I resolve never to take my own life, though tempting thoughts may visit me in times of melancholy and introspection. I pray for deliverance from such temptations and for the strength to go on living.

Anne-Grace struggled with her own thoughts of suicide and made two serious suicide attempts. Then her mother killed herself. Having experienced the aftermath of her mother's suicide, Anne-Grace says:

> I'm alive because of my mother's death. She taught me that in spite of my illness I had to live. Suicide just isn't worth it. . . . I will not, cannot,

end my life as my mother did. . . . [My mother] taught me the most valuable lesson of my life: no matter how bad the pain is, it's never so bad that suicide is the only answer. It's never so bad that the only escape is a false one.[8]

Survivors of suicide are not doomed to repeat the patterns of our loved ones. Their suicides can actually strengthen our resolve and commitment to life. When we are tempted by suicide, we must tell ourselves, *Suicide is not an option for me.*

Jessica's father died from suicide. Later in life Jessica was dying of cancer. As she was suffering, friends suggested that she could take a lethal overdose of certain drugs to end her pain. She adamantly refused, saying that she would not take the route her father did to escape her illness. Jessica did not want to give her children the message that suicide is an acceptable way to go. Instead she chose to let the disease take its course and died from the cancer, setting an opposite example to her father's suicide. Jessica's decision made a lasting impression on her son, who told me that even though he may struggle with depression, he will follow his mother's path and not his grandfather's.

Scripture gives us one key example of suicide prevention. The book of Acts records that the apostle Paul was imprisoned in Philippi during his second missionary journey. An earthquake freed him and the other prisoners. The jailer in charge would have been held responsible for their escape.

Acts 16:27-28 says, "The jailer woke up, and when he saw the prison doors open, he drew his sword and was about to kill himself because he thought the prisoners had escaped. But Paul shouted, 'Don't harm yourself! We are all here!'" Paul subsequently led the jailer to Christ, and his whole household became Christians.

Paul's model of suicide prevention is one we can follow today. He intervened in the jailer's crisis. He stopped him from harming himself. He gave him a reason to live. We can do the same.

If we know of others who are despairing of life, we, like Paul, can call out to them, "Don't harm yourself! We are all here!" We need to show them that we are in fact here for them. We are here, your loved ones, friends and family members, and we don't want you to harm yourself.

Becoming Wounded Healers

Often a traumatic experience becomes an opportunity for later ministry to others. For example, Nixon aide Charles Colson was imprisoned for his involvement in Watergate. Out of that experience grew a sense of calling to minister to prisoners, a vision that eventually developed into the ministry of Prison Fellowship. Many who have lost children or spouses are able to console and comfort others in similar situations. Likewise, many suicide survivors transform their experience by reaching out to others.

As Henri Nouwen says in his book *The Wounded Healer,* understanding our own pain enables us to offer our painful experiences as a source of healing to others.[9] Our woundedness gives us the opportunity to help others who have experienced similar pain. Writes one author, "God will use what you and I have gone through to help others find healing and deliverance from the wounds that still bring pain to their souls."[10]

This does not mean that survivors of suicide just glibly tell others, "Oh, I know how you feel. I've been there." It is not that we simply have a point of reference. Rather, our woundedness transforms us into more sensitive people, more aware of the hurts of those around us, more willing to listen and attend to those in crisis. We become more understanding of those in grief, whatever the occasion for loss. We find ourselves more capable of sharing the pain of others, with a greater capacity for empathy and compassion. As one woman puts it, "The more I look at death's ugly face, and the more I confront my own mortality, the more I will know how to help others who are in pain because of death."[11]

One survivor told me that his cousin's suicide has become a teaching opportunity for his children. He and his wife have encouraged their teens to talk to them or someone else if they ever have thoughts about suicide. Likewise, many survivors participate in suicide prevention work; they

> go on to become actively involved in school and church education programs, hoping to raise awareness about suicide and the psychiatric illnesses that can lead to it. Others work at the state and national level to change legislation or to increase funding for suicide prevention programs and related research. All try to redeem some good from the awfulness they have known; and most succeed.[12]

Survivors may or may not end up in ministries related to suicide. Some do become leaders of support groups for survivors. Others may work or volunteer as chaplains, counselors or social workers. But many find a renewed call to serve people in other ways, whether teaching a Sunday school class, volunteering with a youth group or serving as a big brother or big sister to a troubled student. Having felt the sting of death, survivors hope to make a difference in life.

Many suicide survivors have set up fellowships or foundations to work for suicide prevention, or they volunteer in grief recovery support groups and ministries. Thus they remember their loved one in a way that helps others. Such ministries become acts of remembrance and opportunities to redeem the tragedy of suicide. They are also ways of giving back to our communities and the extended human family.

The *Lessons* of Suicide

Yearn for everlasting life with holy desire.
Day by day remind yourself that you are going to die. . . .
And finally, never lose hope in God's mercy.
THE RULE OF ST. BENEDICT

*D*eath by suicide has a lingering effect on survivors, one that may be felt for decades. Long before Frederick Buechner fully came to grips with his father's suicide, suicide had become a recurring theme in his novels. Even well into his seventies, Buechner was still writing books about the lasting impact of his father's death. Buechner's father killed himself in 1936. In 1999 Buechner wrote, "I suppose one way to read my whole life—my religious faith, the books I have written, the friends I have made—is as a search for him."[1]

Not only do suicides linger in the memories of the immediate survivors, they can haunt families from generation to generation. Novelist Amy Tan, author of *The Joy Luck Club,* writes, "For as long as I can remember, my mother talked of killing herself." Sometimes she ran out into traffic; other times she threatened to kill herself with a knife or scissors. It wasn't until Tan was into her thirties that she realized that her mother was haunted by the memory of witnessing her own mother's suicide. "Thereafter some part of her would always remain the 9-year-old who believed that the only escape from any kind of unhappiness was the route her mother took, an immediate departure from this world to a heavenly form of China."[2] Tan was relieved when her mother died a natural death in old age rather than by her own hand, but she feels yet today the impact of her grandmother's suicide over seventy-five years ago.

"Suicides have a way of haunting the next generation," agrees poet Kathleen Norris. When Norris was twelve years old, she came across an old family photo and saw a face she didn't recognize. She asked about it and heard the story of her Aunt Mary. Norris had never met her aunt; Mary had died the year Norris was born. During her twenties, Mary had become pregnant out of wedlock. A few days after she had her baby, in postpartum despair, she jumped out of a state mental hospital's window.

As Norris reached her twenties, she felt a kindredness with her lost aunt. For a while Norris wrote vaguely suicidal poems about wanting to evaporate like water on the surface of a lake. Trying to understand her aunt's suicide was a factor that led Norris back to church and eventually into a renewed relationship with God. Norris writes, "I believe I became a writer in order to tell her story and possibly redeem it."[3] Her spiritual writings have led many to a deeper understanding of the God of Jesus Christ, and perhaps in that way Norris has indeed redeemed her aunt's story.

As the years pass, we come to realize that we may have learned some things about life through experiencing a suicide. They may be of value not only to ourselves but to others around us as well.

1. *Suicide reminds us that we live in a fallen world.* "Suicide testifies to life's tragic brokenness."[4] It reminds us that this world is not the way it was intended to be. While watching the evening news, my dad once challenged me, "Why are there hurricanes? If there is a God, then why are all these people without their homes?"

I responded, "It's a broken world. In an ideal world, there wouldn't be hurricanes."

Christians believe that the world in its present state is not the way God planned for it to be. God's original plan was for a world without hurricanes, without suicide, where nobody would ever despair of living. But things have become broken along the way. That's not God's fault; it's the fault of a flawed humanity and the workings of evil.

But that's not the end of the story. God is at work redeeming the world, fixing what has been broken. Ultimately God will restore the world and bring about a new heaven and new earth, where there is no longer any suffering, no more pain, no more natural disasters, no more medical traumas. People will no longer face depression or despair, and suicide will never claim someone's life ever again. This is the promise of the Christian story.

So while suicide reminds us that life is broken, God reminds us that he is at work putting things back together, restoring them to the way they were intended to be.

2. *Suicide teaches us that life is uncertain.* Suicide usually occurs suddenly and shockingly. Even when the suicide victim had been depressed for a long period of time, the act of suicide itself brings an abrupt disruption to our existence.

A personal tragedy such as suicide challenges our presumptions about the nature of life. Before the suicide, we may have lived with an unconscious expectation that we are generally in control of our lives. Western society encourages me to believe that I am the master of my fate, the captain of my soul.

But this is not true. In a cosmic sense, what certainty do we have that life will be rosy? What reasonable expectation do we have that a life of ease, comfort and lack of disturbance should be normative? After a suicide, we realize that life is not so definite. On the contrary, life is uncertain. We have no guarantee that our lives will be as we envision them. We are subject to tragedy, reversals of fortune, loss of lives. Life is uncertain, for we are ultimately not in control.

Yet this points us toward the things that hold more certainty. It's unrealistic for us to believe that our life will be spared significant loss or trauma. We recognize our finitude. But this helps us rely on that which is infinite. If we lack control of our own destiny, then we must rely on the only One who has ultimate control of destiny and life itself. The uncertainty of life requires us to anchor ourselves to that which cannot be shaken by the winds and waves of this earthly existence. We must cling to the God of the universe, the only being who transcends the uncertainties of life.

3. *Suicide reminds us of our mortality.* Many of us live from day to day with unspoken illusions of immortality. Death is regularly depicted in movies, TV shows and the six o' clock news, but somehow these images seem unreal. We have a vast disconnect between the fictionalized stories of those who die and real-life people facing death. For the most part, we go through daily life with a presumption that we will live to see tomorrow.

A suicide, or any bereavement, raises the specter of death in our otherwise routine life. Suddenly we are confronted with the reality that our own lives are limited, our own days are numbered. After all, this person we once counted among the living is now among the dead. Can any of us be far behind?

This life is short. Psalm 90 says that the length of our years is seventy, eighty if we have the strength. Many suicides occur at a much earlier age than this, but those who live to a ripe old age still die. The simple truth is that all of us are like grass, soon to wither and fade.

Suicide forces us to grapple with our own mortality. After my father's death, my mother became much more aware of her eventual death and began making plans for her inevitable passing. She wrote up a will, because my father had not had one. She got a safety deposit box at the bank and put important papers and information there, and she sent me all the information about where everything was. Prior to the suicide, she had not pressured Ellen and me to have children, but shortly afterward she began to say things like "Don't wait too long to have children." Her unspoken regret was that my dad had not lived to see any grandchildren, and she was concerned that she might die before we had any kids.

When my father was in his early fifties, his father, my paternal grandfather, died of natural causes. I remember seeing a change in my father in the years following. He became more concerned for his health, less concerned about trivial matters. Perhaps that was part of being in midlife; seeing his father's deteriorating health made him more conscious of his own. After his own stroke and debilitation, he must have been acutely aware of the possibility of impending death.

An acquaintance of mine lost her father just a few months before I lost mine. She remarked that after her father's death, she felt she had aged twenty years. I was only twenty-five when my father died, and as a result my illusions of eternal youth and health disappeared quickly. The death of someone close to us often encourages us to take stock and re-examine our lives.

It is often said that every person attending a funeral thinks not only about the deceased but of their own funeral as well. When will it be? Who will show up? What will others say about me? Whenever we are confronted with death, we are challenged to reconsider our own lives and to live wisely in light of our mortality.

Paul's first letter to Timothy reminds him that God alone is immortal (1 Timothy 6:16) and that he "gives life to everything" (6:13). Our reckoning with our mortality should encourage us to place our hope in the immortal God who calls us to eternal life (6:12).

4. *Suicide shows us the interconnectedness of humanity.* My father was a very private man. He didn't have many friends, rarely went to social functions and wrote few Christmas cards. So I was amazed at how many people came to his funeral and sent condolences. Far more lives had intersected with my father's than I had ever imagined.

I was also surprised at the number of cards I received, from friends, coworkers, relatives, church members, college professors, some folks I had not heard from for years, as well as people I had met recently and didn't know very well. I received a personal sympathy letter from the president of InterVarsity Christian Fellowship, the parent organization of my company.

The ripple effects of a suicide (or any death) are far reaching. We often take our webs of relationships for granted. We are built into networks of friendships and families, and all of us are part of the larger family of humanity. A tragedy like suicide shows us just how many lives an individual life can touch.

We are not isolated individuals; we are part of communities. No one is an island. "The lives of fellow citizens may be bound together in such a way that all are aggrieved by the death of one."[5] Death reminds us to love our neighbors and care for our loved ones while we can, for the day will come when they are no longer with us.

As Henri Nouwen would say, all of us on this planet are on a pilgrimage that takes us from birth to death. "We are not alone; beyond the differences that separate us, we share one common humanity and thus belong to each other."[6]

5. *Suicide demonstrates the necessity of hope.* Our loved one, whatever the immediate circumstances, turned to suicide because of a loss of hope. At some fundamental level he or she came to the conclusion that this life was not worth living. This illustrates something that we normally do not articulate: in order to continue living from day to day, we need to believe that life is worth living. Suicide shows us through negative example that every human heart longs for a reason to live.

In junior high, for a school assignment, I interviewed my father and wrote up a biographical sketch of him. One of the questions I asked was what his purpose in life was. He said that the meaning of life was to make life a little bit better for the next generation. While I thought this noble at the time, it now seems frightfully insufficient.

Perhaps the remarkable thing is that suicide is not more prevalent than it is, given the numbers of disaffected people who wander through life with no clear sense of meaning or purpose. A more stark way of putting it is to ask, Why don't more people take the path of suicide? What keeps us going? Why do we get up in the morning? Ultimately we need to have a purpose for life. Otherwise we may . very well agree with those who choose suicide that life is utterly meaningless.

The Christian story tells us that we do have a purpose for living, that Jesus gives us hope. The resurrection of Jesus was a declaration to human history that death is not the end. As a traditional Easter liturgy declares, "By dying he destroyed our death; by rising he restored our life."

Though this world is subject to decay, God is at work through Jesus to restore his fallen creation. We have hope to carry on because the end is in view. Death does not have the final word. Every breath we take points us to the Giver of life and a life beyond in which every tear will be wiped away and death will be no more.

God made this series of promises to his people through the prophet Isaiah:

> I will lead the blind by ways they have not known,
>   along unfamiliar paths I will guide them;
> I will turn the darkness into light before them
>   and make the rough places smooth.
> These are the things I will do;
>   I will not forsake them. (Isaiah 42:16)

We may be blinded by our grief and loss, but God promises to lead us. The paths following a suicide are unfamiliar, but God will guide us. The way may be dark and rough, but God is with us to provide light and shelter. Above all, though we walk through the valley of the shadow of death, God will not forsake us. We will fear no evil, for God is with us. And we will dwell in the house of the Lord forever.

Epilogue

Going On

Brokenness is not the end of the story. Our pain is deep, but it is not all-encompassing; our loss is enormous, but it is not eternal; and death is our enemy but it does not have the final word.
RUTH PADILLA ELDRENKAMP

My company sent a tree to my father's funeral instead of flowers. At first I was amused, thinking, *Our coworkers sent us a tree! What are we going to do with a tree?* We brought the tree home with us, thinking that it wouldn't stand a chance. My wife and I are notorious plant-killers. When people give us plants or flowers, we can hardly keep them alive. Usually they perish in days.

Several years later, the tree is still alive and well. Even when we forget to water it for weeks at a time, it continues on. Life is surprising like that.

A month after my father's suicide, the movie *Titanic* dominated that year's Academy Awards, winning eleven Oscars including Best Picture. Moviegoers across the nation and around the world were moved by this film, transfixed by the depiction of a love so compelling that it transcends death itself.

It also won the award for Best Song, "My Heart Will Go On," written by James Horner and performed by Celine Dion. The song encapsulates several of the major themes of the movie, including perseverance after loss and the eternal nature of true love. Its haunting melody and poignant lyrics articulate both the grief of tragedy and the resolve to honor the memory of the loved one.

My dad never saw *Titanic*. He had already suffered his stroke by the time of the movie's release and was probably too depressed to venture out. I'm not sure he would have wanted to see it even if he had been well.

Those of us who have experienced the suicide of a loved one are like the survivors of the *Titanic*. Our lives are irrevocably divided into "before" and "after." It is something that we will never forget, a tragedy that will affect us for the rest of our lives.

History tells us that some of the real-life survivors of the *Titanic* were so traumatized that their own lives eventually self-destructed in depression and in some cases suicide.[1] May we not be like them. Though we grieve, we must not compound the tragedy by letting ourselves fall victim to the same demons that claimed our loved one.

Instead we can cultivate an attitude of remembrance. Our hearts will go on. And as long as we go on, we will honor the memory of those who are no longer with us.

Some astute Christians have interpreted the movie *Titanic* as an allegory for the gospel of Jesus Christ. The story is essentially one of conversion and transformation. Early on in the movie, Jack saves Rose from a suicide attempt. Rose's life is so changed by Jack's love for her that she becomes a new person. The sinking of the *Titanic* could be a metaphor for her baptism. She enters the water one person and comes out another. She even takes on a new identity, bearing the name of the one who died to save her.[2]

So it is in the Christian story. As Christians, we bear the name of the Christ who died for us. For Christians, life comes out of death. We live in hope of resurrection. Even though our lives are scarred by death, God is able to bring us out of despair so we can discover new life in him. This is possible only because of the work of Jesus, who willingly gave up his own life so that we might live. He subsequently rose from the grave, defeating death and promising that we can do the same. Because he lives, we can face tomorrow.

As this book was being completed, my wife and I celebrated the birth of our first child, Josiah Alexander. Someday we will tell him about the grandfather he has never known. Though we are sad that they never got a chance to meet each other, we are confident that my dad would have been proud of Josiah and happy to know him.

We will remind our son that even though suicide is a tragedy, God gives us hope and a reason to live. Someday we will see a new heaven and a new earth where death is swallowed up in victory and we shall never grieve again.

Acknowledgments

Thanks first to all those who provided comfort and support to my family during our grief. Your help and assistance was deeply appreciated. I also offer thanks to the fellow suicide survivors—friends and strangers alike—who contributed to this project and provided input and feedback. Thank you for helping me find my way.

Thanks also to our friends at the Christian Church of Clarendon Hills. Our pastoral staff couple, Matthew and Kim Rogers, drove from Illinois to Minnesota and back again to be with us at my father's funeral—on Matthew's birthday. Thank you for being with us that day and for your continued care and friendship.

I am tremendously grateful for our many friends and colleagues at InterVarsity Press, for their community and friendship in times both good and bad. It is a joy and a privilege to work alongside you all. Much thanks in particular to Jeff Crosby, who convinced me of the need for this book, Andy Le Peau, who encouraged me to write it, and Cindy Bunch, whose editorial partnership brought it to fruition.

I am most thankful for my wife and best friend, Ellen, who has been with me every step of this journey. More than anything else, your love and companionship sustained me through the grief process. Thank you.

Appendix
Resources for Suicide Survivors & Suicide Prevention

Nonprofit Organizations

American Association of Suicidology
4201 Connecticut Ave., NW, Suite 408
Washington, DC 20008
202-237-2280; fax 202-237-2282
www.suicidology.org
Dedicated to the understanding and prevention of suicide, AAS promotes research, public awareness programs, education and training for professionals and volunteers. Serves as a national clearinghouse for information on suicide. Its website includes a national directory of support groups for survivors of suicide, listed by state, as well as contact info for crisis centers and hotlines.

American Foundation for Suicide Prevention
120 Wall Street, 22nd Floor
New York, NY 10005
212-363-3500 or 888-333-AFSP; fax 212-363-6237
e-mail: inquiry@afsp.org
www.afsp.org
The American Foundation for Suicide Prevention aims to advance our knowl-

edge of suicide and our ability to prevent it. Website provides helpful data on suicide and resources for prevention.

National Hopeline Network
800-SUICIDE (800-784-2433)
www.hopeline.com
Founded by a survivor after the suicide of his wife. Connects callers to national crisis centers and suicide prevention hotlines through one toll-free phone number.

SAVE: Suicide Awareness Voices of Education
7317 Cahill Road, Suite 207
Minneapolis, MN 55439-0507
952-946-7998 or 888-511-SAVE
e-mail: save@winternet.com
www.save.org
Launched by a couple who lost two children to suicide. Sponsors suicide prevention campaigns with billboards and ads about the danger of untreated depression. Provides suicide prevention kits for schools and organizations.

SOLOS: Survivors of Loved Ones' Suicides
P.O. Box 592
Dumfries, VA 22026-0592
703-580-8958
e-mail: solos@1000deaths.com
www.1000deaths.com
Provides help and support to survivors of suicide through outreach, education and research. Website includes poetry and prose by survivors. The website's domain name comes from the saying "A suicide dies once. Those left behind die a thousand deaths trying to understand why."

SOSR: Survivors of Suicide Web Ring
www.webring.org/cgi-bin/webring?home&ring=sos
Links to other websites by and for survivors of suicide.

Survivors of Suicide
www.thewebpager.com/sos/
Hosts a discussion board where survivors can post messages and help one another. Intent is to offer a safe place to share and discuss the feelings associated with such a loss.

Suicide Prevention Advocacy Network
5034 Odin's Way
Marietta, GA 30068
888-649-1366; fax 770-642-1419
www.spanusa.org
SPAN USA is a nonprofit organization dedicated to the creation of an effective national suicide prevention strategy. SPAN links the energy of those bereaved by suicide with the expertise of leaders in science, business, government and public service to achieve the goal of significantly reducing the national rate of suicide by the year 2010.

Yellow Ribbon Suicide Prevention Program
P.O. Box 644
Westminster, CO 80036-0644
303-429-3530; fax 303-426-4496
e-mail: ask4help@yellowribbon.org
www.yellowribbon.org
The Light for Life Foundation International focuses on preventing teen suicide. The founders started the Yellow Ribbon program in 1994 after their teen took his life just seven minutes before his parents came home and found him. They started making Yellow Ribbon cards for teens which read: "This Ribbon Is a Lifeline! It carries the message that there are those who care and will help! If you are in need and don't know how to ask for help, take this card to a counselor, teacher, clergy, parent or friend and say, 'I NEED TO USE MY YELLOW RIBBON.'" On the back is information to help the friend get help. Over 2.5 million Yellow Ribbon cards have been distributed, and over 1,500 lives have been saved.

U.S. Government Resources for Suicide Prevention

National Strategy for Suicide Prevention
www.mentalhealth.org/suicideprevention/index.htm
Surgeon General David Satcher's call for action on suicide established this collaborative effort between the Substance Abuse and Mental Health Services Administration, the Centers for Disease Control and Prevention, the National Institutes of Health and the Health Resources and Services Administration. This site has links to various agencies with resources for suicide prevention. The Surgeon General's Call to Action to Prevent Suicide (1999) is available on this site.

National Center for Injury Prevention and Control
Mailstop K60
4770 Buford Highway
Atlanta, GA 30341-3724
770-488-4362; fax 770-488-4349
e-mail: OHCINFO@cdc.gov
www.cdc.gov/ncipc/

National Institutes of Mental Health
6001 Executive Blvd., Rm. 8184, MSC 9663
Bethesda, MD 20892-9663
301-443-4513; fax 301-443-4279
e-mail: nimhinfo@nih.gov
www.nimh.nih.gov/research/suicide.htm
Both these organizations provide current statistical data, research and analysis
on suicide, as well as suicide prevention guidelines and resources.

International Organizations

Befrienders International
26/27 Market Place
Kingston upon Thames
Surrey KT1 1JH
United Kingdom
+44-0-20-8541-4949; fax: +44-0-20-8549-1544
e-mail: jo@befrienders.org
www.befrienders.org
Founded in 1974, Befrienders International is a global suicide prevention network with 357 member centers in 41 countries and a head office in London. Its multilingual website features a comprehensive directory of emotional first-aid help lines in countries around the globe. Befrienders aims to reduce suicide by increasing general awareness of suicide, promoting relevant research and establishing volunteer crisis centers.

The Samaritans
10 The Grove
Slough, Berkshire SL1 1QP
United Kingdom
01753-216500; fax 01753-775787
e-mail: jo@samaritans.org

www.samaritans.org.uk
The Samaritans is a registered charity based in the United Kingdom and Republic of Ireland that provides confidential emotional support to any person who is suicidal or despairing. It works to increase public awareness of issues surrounding suicide and depression.

World Health Organization
Avenue Appia 20
1211 Geneva 27
Switzerland
+00-41-22-791-21-11; fax +00-41-22-791-3111
Telex 415-416
e-mail: info@who.int
www.who.int/mental_health/Suicide
In 1999 the World Health Organization launched SUPRE, a worldwide initiative for the prevention of suicide. Its website has data on suicide as a global phenomenon as well as suicide rates for individual countries. It also has resources for suicide prevention, including documents for physicians, health care workers, media, teachers and survivors. A guide for survivors, "Preventing Suicide: How to Start a Survivors' Group" (Geneva: World Health Organization, 2000), is available online at <www.who.int/mental_health/Suicide/resources.html>.

Notes

Introduction
[1]Carla Fine, *No Time to Say Goodbye* (New York: Doubleday, 1997), p. 36, citing the *Diagnostic and Statistical Manual of Mental Disorders*, 4th ed. (DSM-IV) (Washington, D.C.: American Psychiatric Association, 1994).

Chapter 1: Shock
[1]Carla Fine, *No Time to Say Goodbye* (New York: Doubleday, 1997), p. 37.
[2]Randy Christian, "After a Suicide," *Leadership Journal*, Fall 1997, p. 87.
[3]Stephanie Weber, "Home and Beyond," in *Before Their Time: Adult Children's Experiences of Parental Suicide*, ed. Mary Stimming and Maureen Stimming (Philadelphia: Temple University Press, 1999), p. 7.
[4]"Natalie," in Victoria Alexander, *In the Wake of Suicide* (San Francisco: Jossey-Bass, 1991), p. 25.
[5]Stephen Arterburn and Jack Felton, *More Jesus, Less Religion* (Colorado Springs: Waterbrook, 2000), p. 10.
[6]Gerald Sittser, *A Grace Disguised: How the Soul Grows Through Loss* (Grand Rapids, Mich.: Zondervan, 1996), p. 47.
[7]Fine, *No Time to Say Goodbye*, p. 40.
[8]Ibid., pp. 7-12.

Chapter 2: Turmoil
[1]C. S. Lewis, *A Grief Observed* (New York: Harper & Brothers, 1961), p. 75.
[2]Elisabeth Kübler-Ross, *On Death and Dying* (New York: Macmillan, Touchstone, Collier [various editions exist], 1969). Kübler-Ross's "stages of grief" are more accurately described as psychological methods of preparing for the reality of death. Critics have pointed out that they pertain specifically to cases of terminal illness or the reception of catastrophic news, not general bereavement, though in popular usage they have

been applied much more widely. For a critique of Kübler-Ross's stages, see George Kuykendall, "Care for the Dying: A Kübler-Ross Critique," *Theology Today* 38 (April 1981): 37-48 <http://theologytoday.ptsem.edu/apr1981/v38-1-article4.htm>.

[3]Granger E. Westberg, *Good Grief* (Philadelphia: Fortress, 1962).

[4]Gerald Sittser, *A Grace Disguised: How the Soul Grows Through Loss* (Grand Rapids, Mich.: Zondervan, 1996), pp. 50-51.

[5]Mel Laurenz and Daniel Green, *Overcoming Grief and Trauma* (Grand Rapids, Mich.: Baker, 1995), pp. 29, 31.

[6]Lewis, *Grief Observed*, p. 19.

[7]Carla Fine, *No Time to Say Goodbye* (New York: Doubleday, 1997), p. 40.

[8]Stephanie Ericsson, *Companion Through the Darkness* (New York: HarperCollins, 1993), pp. 89-90.

[9]Kay Redfield Jamison, *Night Falls Fast* (New York: Alfred A. Knopf, 1999), p. 300.

[10]Victoria Alexander, *In the Wake of Suicide* (San Francisco: Jossey-Bass, 1991), p. 81.

[11]Iris Bolton, in Jamison, *Night Falls Fast*, p. 296.

[12]Judith Felts Meade, "The Journey of Loss and the Quest for Healing After Losing a Client to Suicide," *Family Therapy News*, February/March 2001, pp. 24-25.

[13]Alexander, *In the Wake of Suicide*, p. 134.

[14]"Joan," in ibid., pp. 61, 66-67.

[15]Fine, *No Time to Say Goodbye*, p. 91.

[16]Ibid., p. 95.

[17]Ibid., p. 91.

[18]Jamison reports that one-third of surviving family members say they feel stigmatized by suicide (*Night Falls Fast*, p. 294).

[19]Margaret Atwood, *The Blind Assassin* (New York: Doubleday, 2000), p. 473.

[20]Phillip Lopate, "Suicide of a Schoolteacher," in *On Suicide*, ed. John Miller (San Francisco: Chronicle, 1992), p. 28.

[21]Ericsson, *Companion Through the Darkness*, p. 91.

[22]Fine, *No Time to Say Goodbye*, p. 200.

[23]Lopate, "Suicide of a Schoolteacher," p. 21.

[24]Jamison, *Night Falls Fast*, p. 296.

[25]Ibid., p. 293. Jamison cites a study in which one in ten family members admitted relief. A higher percentage probably experience relief but are unwilling to admit it.

[26]Eric Marcus, *Why Suicide?* (San Francisco: HarperSanFrancisco, 1996), p. 130.

[27]Recent studies find higher rates of suicide and suicidal behavior in suicide survivors and family members of those who attempt suicide. "Those who commit suicide are at least two or three times as likely to have a family history of suicide as those who do not" (Jamison, *Night Falls Fast*, p. 169).

[28]Ann Smolin and John Guinan, *Healing After the Suicide of a Loved One* (New York: Simon & Schuster/Fireside, 1993), p. 94.

[29]Ibid., pp. 94-95.

[30]John Hewett, *After Suicide* (Philadelphia: Westminster Press, 1980), pp. 35-36.

[31]Jamison, *Night Falls Fast*, pp. 296, 302.

[32]Ibid., p. 301.

Chapter 3: Lament

[1]Heather Zuzick, "Old at Heart," in *Before Their Time: Adult Children's Experiences of*

Parental Suicide, ed. Mary Stimming and Maureen Stimming (Philadelphia: Temple University Press, 1999), p. 53.

[2]Philip Gulley, *For Everything a Season* (Sisters, Ore.: Multnomah Press, 1999), pp. 94-95.

[3]Stephen Arterburn and Jack Felton, *More Jesus, Less Religion* (Colorado Springs: Waterbrook, 2000), p. 11.

[4]B. R. McCane, "Burial, Mourning," in *Dictionary of New Testament Background,* ed. Craig Evans and Stanley Porter (Downers Grove, Ill.: InterVarsity Press, 2000), pp. 174-75.

[5]Hospice Council of Metropolitan Washington, "A Guide to Grief" brochure (Arlington, Va.: National Hospice Organization), p. 1.

[6]Bob Sheldon, "Carrying On After Suicide," *Bereavement Magazine,* January/February 2000, p. 24.

[7]Gerald Sittser, *A Grace Disguised: How the Soul Grows Through Loss* (Grand Rapids, Mich.: Zondervan, 1996), p. 33.

[8]For example, see Psalms 6, 13, 22, 28, 31, 39, 69. Other examples of lament outside the psalms include David's lament for the deaths of Jonathan and Saul (2 Sam 1:19-27) and David's lament for Absalom (2 Sam 18:33). Jeremiah composed laments at the death of Josiah (2 Chron 35:25).

[9]Walter Brueggemann, foreword to *Psalms of Lament* by Ann Weems (Louisville, Ky.: Westminster John Knox, 1995), p. x.

[10]Barry G. Webb, *Five Festal Garments* (Downers Grove, Ill.: InterVarsity Press, 2001), p. 61.

[11]Amy Plantinga Pauw, "Dying Well," in *Practicing Our Faith,* ed. Dorothy C. Bass (San Francisco: Jossey-Bass, 1997), p. 168.

[12]Diane Ackerman, *A Slender Thread* (New York: Random House, 1997), p. 23.

[13]Gloria Vanderbilt, *A Mother's Story* (New York: Alfred A. Knopf, 1996), p. 116.

[14]Kathleen Norris, *The Cloister Walk* (New York: Riverhead, 1996), p. 281.

[15]Frederick Buechner, *Telling Secrets* (San Francisco: HarperSanFrancisco, 1991), pp. 7-9.

[16]Randy Christian, "After a Suicide," *Leadership Journal,* Fall 1997, p. 86.

[17]Ibid.

[18]John Hewett, *After Suicide* (Philadelphia: Westminster Press, 1980), p. 69.

[19]Ann Smolin and John Guinan, *Healing After the Suicide of a Loved One* (New York: Simon & Schuster/Fireside, 1993), p. 107.

[20]Kay Redfield Jamison, *Night Falls Fast* (New York: Alfred A. Knopf, 1999), p. 303.

[21]Buechner, *Telling Secrets,* pp. 34-35, 99-100; see also Frederick Buechner, *The Wizard's Tide* (San Francisco: Harper, 1990).

[22]Nicholas Wolterstorff, *Lament for a Son* (Grand Rapids, Mich.: Eerdmans, 1987), p. 6.

[23]Ibid., p. 89.

[24]Pauw, "Dying Well," p. 168.

Chapter 4: Relinquishment

[1]Henri Nouwen, *Our Greatest Gift* (San Francisco: HarperSanFrancisco, 1994), pp. 26-27.

[2]Ibid., p. 48.

[3]Joseph Cardinal Bernardin, *The Gift of Peace* (Chicago: Loyola University Press,

1997), pp. 127-28.

[4]Ibid., p. x.

[5]C. S. Lewis writes, "For all pairs of lovers without exception, bereavement is a universal and integral part of our experience of love. It follows marriage as normally as marriage follows courtship or as autumn follows summer. It is not a truncation of the process but one of its phases; not the interruption of the dance, but the next figure" (*A Grief Observed* [New York: Harper & Brothers, 1961], p. 68).

[6]George Kuykendall, "Care for the Dying: A Kübler-Ross Critique," *Theology Today* 38 (April 1981): 45 <http://theologytoday.ptsem.edu/apr1981/v38-1-article4.htm>.

[7]Nicholas Wolterstorff, *Lament for a Son* (Grand Rapids, Mich.: Eerdmans, 1987), p. 63.

[8]Alister McGrath, *The Journey* (New York: Doubleday, 2000), p. 109.

[9]Wolterstorff, *Lament for a Son*, p. 63.

[10]Kuykendall, "Care for the Dying," p. 46.

[11]Cornelius Plantinga Jr., *Not the Way It's Supposed to Be* (Grand Rapids, Mich.: Eerdmans, 1995), p. 10.

[12]I am indebted to New Testament professor Christopher Davis, Minnesota Bible College, Rochester, for this insight.

Chapter 5: Remembrance

[1]Evangelical Lutheran Church in America, "A Message on Suicide Prevention," Department for Studies, Division for Church in Society (November 1999), p. 8, <www.elca.org/dcs/suicide_prevention.html>.

[2]Douglas Connelly, *After Life* (Downers Grove, Ill.: InterVarsity Press, 1995), p. 52.

[3]Grief therapist Victor Parachin, quoted in Kenn Filkins, *Comfort Those Who Mourn* (Joplin, Mo.: College Press, 1992), p. 149.

[4]M. Craig Barnes, *When God Interrupts* (Downers Grove, Ill.: InterVarsity Press, 1996), p. 9.

[5]Kay Redfield Jamison, *Night Falls Fast* (New York: Alfred A. Knopf, 1999), p. 294.

[6]Leland Ryken, James C. Wilhoit and Tremper Longman III, eds. *Dictionary of Biblical Imagery* (Downers Grove, Ill: InterVarsity Press, 1998), p. 702.

[7]R. S. Hess, "Noah," in *New Dictionary of Biblical Theology,* ed. T. Desmond Alexander and Brian S. Rosner (Downers Grove, Ill: InterVarsity Press, 2000), p. 679.

[8]C. S. Lewis, *A Grief Observed* (New York: Harper & Brothers, 1961), p. 36.

[9]Ibid., pp. 73-74.

[10]Ibid., p. 42.

[11]Ibid., p. 58.

[12]Ibid., pp. 85-86.

[13]Gerald Sittser, *A Grace Disguised: How the Soul Grows Through Loss* (Grand Rapids, Mich.: Zondervan, 1996), pp. 111-12.

[14]Carla Fine, *No Time to Say Goodbye* (New York: Doubleday, 1997), p. 196.

Chapter 6: Why Did This Happen?

[1]Kay Redfield Jamison, *Night Falls Fast* (New York: Alfred A. Knopf, 1999), p. 295.

[2]Ibid., p. 198.

[3]Ibid., pp. 333, 75-78.

[4]From a CDC report published in 1994 to help media coverage of suicides be more

responsible, quoted in ibid., p. 280.

[5]Massachusetts Department of Youth Services, cited by Catherine Clark Kroeger and Nancy Nason-Clark, *No Place for Abuse* (Downers Grove, Ill.: InterVarsity Press, 2001), p. 83.

[6]A Harvard Medical School study cited in "Marital Failures Spawn Suicides," *Current Thoughts and Trends,* February 2001, p. 7.

[7]Anna Mulrine, "Where Do Hopes Go?" *U.S. News & World Report,* May 7, 2001, p. 43.

[8]National Institute of Mental Health statistics, fact sheet <www.nimh.nih.gov/research/suicide/faq.cfm>.

[9]Eric Westervelt, "Police Suicides," *Morning Edition,* National Public Radio, August 9, 2001. In the year 2000, 418 U.S. police officers died of suicide while just 150 were killed in the line of duty. See also the National Police Suicide Foundation website <www.psf.org>.

[10]Eric Marcus, *Why Suicide?* (San Francisco: HarperSanFrancisco, 1996), pp. 20-21.

[11]American Foundation for Suicide Prevention <www.afsp.org/about/depresfc.htm>.

[12]William Styron, quoting himself in *Darkness Visible* (New York: Vintage, 1990), p. 33.

[13]Jamison, *Night Falls Fast,* p. 39.

[14]American Foundation for Suicide Prevention <www.afsp.org/about/manicdep.htm>.

[15]Alan L. Berman, "Suicide," in Microsoft Encarta Encyclopedia 99 (Redmond, Wash.: Microsoft Corporation, 1999), CD-ROM.

[16]Martha Ainsworth, "If You Are Thinking About Suicide . . . Read This First," <www.metanoia.org/suicide/spagebw.htm>.

[17]Robert D. Putnam, *Bowling Alone: The Collapse and Revival of American Community* (New York: Simon & Schuster, 2000), p. 262.

[18]Denise Mann, "Suicide Risk Does Not Go Up During Holidays," posted on WebMD Medical News (December 26, 2000) <http://my.webmd.com/condition_center_content/dep/article/1728.67796>. In my previous book I mistakenly perpetuated this myth by saying that more suicides take place on Valentine's Day than any other day except Christmas (Albert Y. Hsu, *Singles at the Crossroads: A Fresh Perspective on Christian Singleness* [Downers Grove, Ill.: InterVarsity Press, 1997], p. 170). Consider this an official retraction.

[19]According to the American Foundation for Suicide Prevention, the month with the highest suicide rates is actually April.

[20]Michael Eaton, "Ecclesiastes," in *The New Bible Commentary,* ed. D. A. Carson et al., 4th ed. (Downers Grove, Ill.: InterVarsity Press, 1994), p. 609.

[21]Charles Colson and Nancy Pearcey, *How Now Shall We Live?* (Wheaton, Ill.: Tyndale House, 1999), pp. 260-61.

[22]Dietrich Bonhoeffer, *Ethics* (New York: Macmillan, 1955), p. 167.

[23]American Foundation for Suicide Prevention, "Creativity, Depression and Suicide" <www.afsp.org/depress/creative.htm>.

[24]Kathleen Norris, *The Virgin of Bennington* (New York: Riverhead, 2001), p. 185.

[25]Styron, *Darkness Visible,* pp. 35-36.

[26]Studies have found that scientists, composers and top businessmen are five times more likely to kill themselves than the general population and that writers and poets showed very high suicide rates as well (Jamison, *Night Falls Fast,* pp. 180-81). Jamison's list of artistic suicide casualties is found on pp. 365-87.

[27]Anna Mulrine, "Another Victim, 3 Months Later," *U.S. News & World Report,* December

24, 2001, p. 7.

[28]Colleen Slevin, "Columbine Suicide: Mother of Victims Shoots Self in Pawn Shop," Associated Press wire story, October 22, 1999.

[29]Tom Weir, "Some of Us Are Still Hurting," *USA Today,* May 10, 2000, p. 3C.

[30]Odhiambo Okite, "Peace Worker's Suicide a Wake-Up Call for Churches," *Anglican Journal,* October 2000, p. 9.

[31]Johann Christoph Arnold, *Why Forgive?* (Farmington, Penn.: Plough, 2000), p. 6.

[32]Henri Nouwen, *The Return of the Prodigal Son* (New York: Doubleday/Image, 1994), p. 50.

[33]Douglas Webster, *The Discipline of Surrender* (Downers Grove, Ill.: InterVarsity Press, 2001), p. 83.

[34]Margaret Atwood, *The Blind Assassin* (New York: Doubleday, 2000), p. 494.

[35]Phillip Lopate, "Suicide of a Schoolteacher," in *On Suicide,* ed. John Miller (San Francisco: Chronicle, 1992), p. 18.

[36]Iris Bolton, in Jamison, *Night Falls Fast,* p. 297.

[37]I have borrowed this analogy from Nick Pollard, *Evangelism Made Slightly Less Difficult* (Downers Grove, Ill.: InterVarsity Press, 1998), p. 132.

[38]Becca Cowan Johnson, *Good Guilt, Bad Guilt* (Downers Grove, Ill.: InterVarsity Press, 1996), p. 21.

[39]John Hewett, *After Suicide* (Philadelphia: Westminster Press, 1980), pp. 75-76.

Chapter 7: Is Suicide the Unforgivable Sin?

[1]Eric Marcus, *Why Suicide?* (San Francisco: HarperSanFrancisco, 1996), p. 9.

[2]Kay Redfield Jamison, *Night Falls Fast* (New York: Alfred A. Knopf, 1999), p. 14.

[3]Augustine *City of God* 1.17. Modern interpreters have challenged this view, pointing out that the second half of the Ten Commandments consists of a catalog of sins *against one's neighbor.* They are concerned with our duty to others, that we do not steal from others or take a neighbor's spouse as our own. The sixth commandment is a command not to kill our neighbor. While it may have an indirect application to suicide, it is not a *direct* prohibition of killing oneself. See Robert N. Wennberg, *Terminal Choices* (Grand Rapids, Mich.: Eerdmans, 1989), pp. 56-57.

[4]Thomas Aquinas, "Fifth Article: Whether It Is Lawful to Kill Oneself?" *Summa Theologica* 2.2.64.5.

[5]Jamison, *Night Falls Fast,* pp. 15-16, 169.

[6]William Shakespeare, *Hamlet,* act 1, scene 2, lines 129-32.

[7]Ibid., act 1, scene 5, lines 75-80 and 11-12.

[8]Ibid., act 3, scene 3, lines 73-78.

[9]Dietrich Bonhoeffer, *Ethics* (New York: Macmillan, 1955), p. 169.

[10]J. Davis McCaughey, "Suicide: Some Theological Considerations," *Theology* 70 (1967): 67, quoted in Wennberg, *Terminal Choices,* p. 55.

[11]Gilbert Meilaender, *Bioethics* (Grand Rapids, Mich.: Eerdmans, 1996), p. 59.

[12]Wennberg, *Terminal Choices,* pp. 47-48.

[13]John C. Roos, letter to the editor, *Christianity Today,* September 4, 2000, p. 23. Original quote says "Paul's list of the 'faithful' in Hebrews 11." I am not convinced that Paul is the author of the anonymous epistle to the Hebrews.

[14]Donal O'Mathuna, "But the Bible Doesn't Say They Were Wrong, Does It?" in *Suicide: A Christian Response,* ed. Timothy J. Demy and Gary P. Stewart (Grand Rapids, Mich.:

Kregel, 1998), pp. 362, 366.

[15]Luke Timothy Johnson, "A Disembodied Theology of the Body," in *Commonweal*, January 26, 2001, p. 16. Johnson's remarks come from a discussion about the morality of birth control, and he argues against an "act-centered morality" that assumes that the use of a contraceptive cancels out an openness to life. "This is simply nonsense," Johnson writes. "The woman who kills in self-defense (or in defense of her children) does not become a murderer." I would contend that many suicides, though not all, should be considered likewise.

[16]A number of evangelical theologians are increasingly open to the possibility that hell does not consist of conscious eternal torment but may eventually lead to complete annihilation instead. See William Crockett, ed., *Four Views on Hell* (Grand Rapids, Mich.: Zondervan, 1992), and Edward Fudge and Robert Peterson, *Two Views of Hell* (Downers Grove, Ill.: InterVarsity Press, 2000). For a proposal for harmonizing traditionalist and annihilationist views of hell, see Gregory Boyd, *Satan and the Problem of Evil* (Downers Grove, Ill.: InterVarsity Press, 2001), chaps. 11-12.

[17]Lewis Smedes, "Is Suicide Unforgivable?" *Christianity Today*, July 10, 2000, p. 61.

[18]United States Catholic Conference, *Catechism of the Catholic Church* (New York: Doubleday/Image, 1994), p. 609. In fact, the catechism says that "the Church prays for persons who have taken their own lives."

[19]Ibid., p. 609.

[20]Meilaender, *Bioethics*, p. 60.

[21]"Tragedy as Plot Motif," in *Dictionary of Biblical Imagery*, ed. Leland Ryken, James C. Wilhoit and Tremper Longman III (Downers Grove, Ill.: InterVarsity Press, 1998), p. 882.

[22]Cornelius Plantinga Jr., *Not the Way It's Supposed to Be* (Grand Rapids, Mich.: Eerdmans, 1995), p. 140.

[23]John White, *The Masks of Melancholy* (Downers Grove, Ill: InterVarsity Press, 1982), p. 147.

[24]Meilaender, *Bioethics*, p. 70.

[25]Wennberg, *Terminal Choices*, p. 50.

[26]Ibid., *Terminal Choices*, pp. 51-52.

[27]Interestingly, in 1646 John Donne wrote a treatise on suicide, *Biathanatos*, in which he confessed his own occasional contemplations of suicide: "Whensoever any affliction assails me, methinks I have the keys of my prison in mine own hand, and no remedy presents itself so soon to my heart as mine own sword" (quoted in Jamison, *Night Falls Fast*, p. 17).

[28]Lauren Winner, "Sympathy for the Devil," Beliefnet.com (February 16, 2000) <www.beliefnet.com/story/11/story_1157.html>.

[29]Gregory A. Boyd and Edward K. Boyd, *Letters from a Skeptic* (Wheaton, Ill.: Victor, 1994), p. 36.

[30]Johann Christoph Arnold, *Why Forgive?* (Farmington, Penn.: Plough, 2000), p. 59.

Chapter 8: Where Is God When It Hurts?

[1]C. S. Lewis, *A Grief Observed* (New York: Harper & Brothers, 1961), p. 23.

[2]Ibid., p. 44.

[3]Jean Améry, *On Suicide*, trans. John D. Barlow (Bloomington: Indiana University Press, 1999), pp. 59-60.

[4]Jürgen Moltmann, *Jesus Christ for Today's World* (Minneapolis: Fortress, 1994), pp. 2-3. Biographical information comes from Stanley J. Grenz and Roger Olson, *Twentieth-Century Theology* (Downers Grove, Ill.: InterVarsity Press, 1992), p. 173.

[5]John C. Cavadini, "No, Not Exactly" (review of Thomas G. Weinandy, *Does God Suffer?*) *Commonweal,* March 9, 2001, pp. 41-42.

[6]Gary Haugen, *Good News About Injustice* (Downers Grove, Ill.: InterVarsity Press, 1999), pp. 78-79.

[7]Moltmann, *Jesus Christ for Today's World,* pp. 38, 40.

[8]Nicholas Wolterstorff, *Lament for a Son* (Grand Rapids, Mich.: Eerdmans, 1987), p. 81.

[9]Moltmann, *Jesus Christ for Today's World,* p. 44.

[10]Ibid., p. 45.

[11]Wolterstorff, *Lament for a Son,* p. 90.

[12]John G. Stackhouse's summary of philosopher Alvin Plantinga's free will defense to the problem of evil, in "Mind over Skepticism," *Christianity Today,* June 11, 2001, p. 74.

[13]Quoted in Lee Strobel, *The Case for Faith* (Grand Rapids, Mich.: Zondervan, 2000), p. 46.

[14]John R. W. Stott, *The Cross of Christ* (Downers Grove, Ill.: InterVarsity Press, 1986), p. 329.

[15]Kazoh Kitamori, *The Theology of the Pain of God* (London: SCM Press, 1966), quoted in Stott, *Cross of Christ,* p. 332.

[16]Seiichi Yagi, "The Third Generation, 1945-1970," in *A History of Japanese Theology,* ed. Yasuo Furuya (Grand Rapids, Mich.: Eerdmans, 1997), p. 88.

[17]Stott, *Cross of Christ,* pp. 335-36.

[18]Godfrey Thring, "Crown Him with Many Crowns."

[19]Stephanie Ericsson, *Companion Through the Darkness* (New York: HarperCollins, 1993), p. 76.

[20]Lewis, *Grief Observed,* pp. 63-64.

[21]Henri Nouwen, *Reaching Out* (New York: Doubleday/Image, 1975), p. 128.

[22]See N. T. Wright, *The Challenge of Jesus* (Downers Grove, Ill.: InterVarsity Press, 1999), chap. 7, especially p. 165. Luke uses certain key words in both passages. In Luke 2:43 Mary and Joseph are "unaware" of Jesus' absence. In Luke 24:16 the Emmaus disciples "were kept from recognizing" Jesus, but in verse 31 their eyes were opened and "they recognized him." The root verbs for "aware" and "to recognize" are the same.

Chapter 9: The Spirituality of Grief

[1]Walter Wangerin, *Mourning into Dancing* (Grand Rapids, Mich.: Zondervan, 1992), p. 147.

[2]Cindy Crosby, *Waiting for Morning* (Grand Rapids, Mich.: Baker, 2001), p. 100.

[3]Gregory A. Boyd, *God at War* (Downers Grove, Ill.: InterVarsity Press, 1997), p. 26.

[4]D. W. Amundsen, "Suffering," in *New Dictionary of Theology,* ed. Sinclair B. Ferguson, David F. Wright and J. I. Packer (Downers Grove, Ill.: InterVarsity Press, 1988), p. 669.

[5]Paul Marshall, *Their Blood Cries Out* (Dallas: Word, 1997), pp. 153-56.

[6]Ruth Padilla Eldrenkamp, address at the 1999 International Fellowship of Evangelical

Students World Assembly in Seoul, South Korea, quoted in Vivienne Stacey, *Mission Ventured* (Leicester, U.K.: Inter-Varsity Press, 2001), p. 188.

[7]Robert V. Rakestraw, "New Dimensions in the Study of Angels and Demons," in *New Dimensions in Evangelical Thought*, ed. David S. Dockery (Downers Grove, Ill.: InterVarsity Press, 1998), p. 281.

[8]C. S. Lewis, *A Grief Observed* (New York: Harper & Brothers, 1961), p. 50.

[9]John Stott, *Romans* (Downers Grove, Ill.: InterVarsity Press, 1994), p. 259.

[10]F. P. Cotterell, "Suffering," in *New Dictionary of Biblical Theology*, ed. T. Desmond Alexander and Brian S. Rosner (Downers Grove, Ill.: InterVarsity Press, 2000), p. 805.

[11]Henri Nouwen, *The Return of the Prodigal Son* (New York: Doubleday/Image, 1994), p. 128.

[12]From the documentary *Abraham and Mary Lincoln: A House Divided*, produced by David Grubin, quoted in Lewis Lord, "There's Something About Mary Todd," *U.S. News & World Report*, February 19, 2001, p. 53.

[13]Nouwen, *Return of the Prodigal Son*, p. 130.

[14]Ken Gire, *Intense Moments with the Savior* (Grand Rapids, Mich.: Zondervan, 1994), p. xii.

[15]Lee Strobel, *What Jesus Would Say* (Grand Rapids, Mich.: Zondervan, 1994), p. 161.

[16]Johann Christoph Arnold, *Why Forgive?* (Farmington, Penn.: Plough, 2000), p. 155.

[17]Lewis, *Grief Observed*, p. 76.

[18]Wangerin, *Mourning into Dancing*, p. 151.

[19]Lewis, *Grief Observed*, p. 79.

Chapter 10: The Healing Community

[1]Nicholas Wolterstorff, *Lament for a Son* (Grand Rapids, Mich.: Eerdmans, 1987), p. 34.

[2]Ibid.

[3]Dale and Juanita Ryan, *Receiving Comfort from God* (Downers Grove, Ill.: InterVarsity Press, 2001), p. 5.

[4]Wolterstorff, *Lament for a Son*, p. 35.

[5]"Compassionate Friends Organization Changes Suicide Language," press release from The Compassionate Friends, Oak Brook, Illinois, March 1999.

[6]Stephen Arterburn and Jack Felton, *More Jesus, Less Religion* (Colorado Springs: Waterbrook, 2000), p. 63.

[7]Eric Marcus, *Why Suicide?* (San Francisco: HarperSanFrancisco, 1996), p. 157.

[8]Anne-Grace Scheinin, quoted in Douglas Connelly, *After Life* (Downers Grove, Ill.: InterVarsity Press, 1995), pp. 54-55.

[9]Henri Nouwen, *The Wounded Healer* (New York: Doubleday/Image, 1972), p. 87.

[10]Frank Peretti, *The Wounded Spirit* (Nashville: Word, 2000), p. 182.

[11]Phyllis Le Peau, *Caring for People in Grief* (Downers Grove, Ill.: InterVarsity Press, 1991), p. 11.

[12]Kay Redfield Jamison, *Night Falls Fast* (New York: Alfred A. Knopf, 1999), p. 307.

Chapter 11: The Lessons of Suicide

[1]Frederick Buechner, *The Eyes of the Heart* (San Francisco: HarperSanFrancisco, 1999), pp. 23-24.

[2]Amy Tan, "Family Ghosts Hoard Secrets That Bewitch the Living," *The New York*

Times, February 26, 2001 <www.nytimes.com/2001/02/26/arts/26TAN.html>. Tan's novel *The Bonesetter's Daughter* (New York: Putnam, 2001) explores some of the ways a suicide affects future generations.

[3]Kathleen Norris, *Dakota* (New York: Houghton Mifflin, 1993), p. 101. Also see Kathleen Norris, *The Virgin of Bennington* (New York: Riverhead, 2001), p. 127.

[4]Evangelical Lutheran Church in America, Department for Studies, Division for Church in Society (November 1999), "Message on Suicide Prevention," p. 1 <www.elca.org/dcs/suicide_prevention.html>.

[5]Gilbert Meilaender, *Bioethics* (Grand Rapids, Mich.: Eerdmans, 1996), p. 61.

[6]Henri Nouwen, *Our Greatest Gift* (San Francisco: HarperSanFrancisco, 1994), p. 27.

Epilogue

[1]At least two survivors of the *Titanic,* Jack Thayer and Frederick Fleet, killed themselves later in life.

[2]Ironically, Rose's former fiancé, Cal Hockley, survived the sinking of the *Titanic* only to kill himself after the stock market crash. If we continue the analogy and see Cal as a symbol of evil or villainy, perhaps this points to the Christian truth that death itself will die.

Index